The Nature of Science

Junior Cycle

Student Resources & Revision

Tim Gill
Claire Grant
Vicky Meredith
Sheena Odongo

MENTOR

MENTOR BOOKS
43 Furze Road
Sandyford Industrial Estate
Dublin 18
Tel: 01-2952112/3
Fax: 01-2952114
Website: www.mentorbooks.ie
Email: admin@mentorbooks.ie

All rights reserved.

Text: Tim Gill
Claire Grant
Vicky Meredith
Sheena Odongo

Edited by: Una Whelan
Treasa O'Mahony
Linda Richardson

Cover design: Mary Byrne

Design & Layout: Mary Byrne

Illustrations: Brian Fitzgerald

Acknowledgements
The publisher would like to thank the following for permission to reproduce material:
Fiona Reddan in *The Irish Times*; Irene Steffens, nutritional therapist; NASA; *National Geographic*; Mars-One; Chocolate 'As good for you as exercise' © Telegraph Media Group Limited 2011; Tim Appenzellar.
   The publisher has made every effort to trace and acknowledge the holders of copyright for material in this book. In the event of any copyright holder having been omitted, the publishers will come to a suitable arrangement at the first opportunity.

ISBN: 978-1-909417-51-9

© Tim Gill, Claire Grant, Vicky Meredith, Sheena Odongo 2016

Contents

Introduction 4

Nature of Science

1. Science in Our World 5
2. Working Safely in a Science Laboratory . 9
3. How Scientists Work 11
4. Scientific Investigations 13
5. Communication and Research in Science . 16
6. Discovery and Invention 18

The Biological World

7. Cell Structure and Function 21
8. Cell Processes: Photosynthesis and Respiration 24
9. The Circulatory System 28
10. Food and the Digestive System 32
11. The Respiratory System 36
12. Reproduction & Genetics 39
13. Reproduction in Humans 43
14. Evolution 46
15. Human Health 49
16. Studying Habitats and their Communities 53
17. Biodiversity 57

The Chemical World

18. Mass and Matter 61
19. Classifying Materials 64
20. Mixtures 67
21. Properties of Materials 70
22. Structure of the Atom 73
23. The Periodic Table and Chemical Formulae 76
24. Acids and Bases 79
25. Chemical Reactions 82
26. Life Cycle of Materials 85

The Physical World

27. Measurements and Units 90
28. Density, Speed and Acceleration 94
29. Force 99
30. Energy 103
31. Electricity 107
32. Electronics 111
33. Technology in Our Lives 114
34. Generating Electricity 117

Earth and Space

35. Our Universe 121
36. Earth and Other Planets 124
37. The Earth, Sun and Moon 126
38. Space Exploration 129
39. Cycles on Earth 132
40. Climate Change 136
41. Energy Sources 143

Introduction

Welcome to **The Nature of Science Student Resources & Revision**. This book contains a variety of resources and activities relating to the key topics on the Junior Cycle Science Specification.

Although the book follows the same chapter order as **The Nature of Science Textbook**, it can be used independently as a useful resource and revision aid.

Each chapter begins with **Review questions** which address the basic information surrounding a key topic from the Science Specification.

Knowledge and Understanding questions follow – these tackle more difficult concepts associated with the key topic.

Many chapters also contain **Analyse and Interpret** sections, containing graphs and data analysis activities.

In addition, **Case Studies** appear frequently. Many of these are taken from media sources, allowing students to see how science is part of the wider world and how reporting on scientific matters should be carefully analysed for bias. These will also help students to develop scientific literacy and numeracy.

Overall, this **Student Resources & Revision** book provides students with the opportunity to enhance their understanding of the relevant topics, to develop key scientific skills and to achieve the learning outcomes of the Junior Cycle Science Specification.

Dedication

This book has been a team effort and we would like to thank everyone at Mentor Books for their guidance and support, especially Danny McCarthy, Treasa O'Mahony and our editor Una Whelan. We are grateful to Mary Byrne for her excellent work in developing the layout and overall design of the book. We would particularly like to offer our gratitude to our families, friends and colleagues for their invaluable support and encouragement throughout this project. Last, but certainly not least, a special thank you to our students for providing us with plenty of inspiration.

Tim Gill
Claire Grant
Vicky Meredith
Sheena Odongo

1 Science in Our World

Look at each photo below and read the question that goes with it. You may not know the exact answer to each question but write what you do know on the lines provided. Pick out the questions that you find most difficult to answer. How do you think you could find out more about how to answer these questions?

1. Why does the moon always look different? ▶

_____
_____
_____
_____

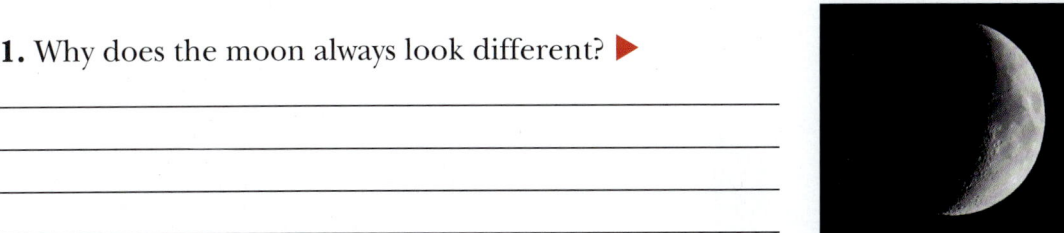

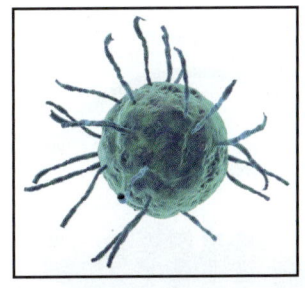

◀ **2.** What is a virus?

_____
_____
_____
_____

3. Why do people have different coloured eyes? ▶

_____
_____
_____
_____

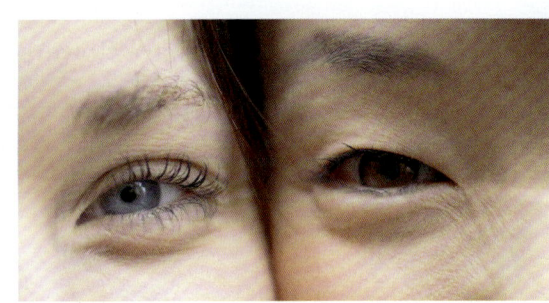

◀ **4.** What causes identical twins?

_____
_____
_____
_____

5. Why do lemons taste so bitter? ▶

_____
_____
_____
_____

The Nature of Science Resources & Revision

6. Why are polar bears white?
_____
_____
_____

7. Why do we see rainbows?
_____
_____
_____
_____

8. What makes plants grow?
_____
_____
_____

9. Why do plants have flowers?
_____
_____
_____

10. How did the universe begin?
_____
_____
_____

11. Why should we recycle?
_____
_____
_____

Science in Our World 1

12. What is the difference between water and ice?
_____
_____
_____
_____

13. What makes things heavy?
_____
_____
_____
_____

14. What is global warming?
_____
_____
_____
_____

15. What is inside an atom?
_____
_____
_____

16. What is inside a fire extinguisher?
_____
_____
_____

17. What do they do on the International Space Station?
_____
_____
_____

7

The Nature of Science **Resources & Revision**

18. How can a big ship made of iron float? ▲

2 Working Safely in a Science Laboratory

Review Questions

1. Study the diagram and answer the following questions.

(a) Identify four hazards in this diagram.
   (i) _____
   (ii) _____
   (iii) _____
   (iv) _____

(b) Identify four precautions that the scientist could take to make this workbench safe.
   (i) _____
   (ii) _____
   (iii) _____
   (iv) _____

2. List two steps that should be taken before beginning an experiment.
   (a) _____
   (b) _____

3. Which piece of safety equipment should always be used when working with chemicals?
   _____

4. Why should you always read the label before collecting a chemical?
   _____

Knowledge and Understanding

1. Name these chemical safety symbols and explain what they mean.

2. Draw a diagram using suitable detail to show a beaker of water being heated.
3. A student is asked to accurately measure 100 cm^3 of water and then heat it to 60°C. Name all of the pieces of equipment that would be needed for this task.
4. List three mistakes that could cause an accident when using a Bunsen burner.
5. List three ways that you can keep the science laboratory safe.
6. Why is it important to tie up long hair in the lab?

3 How Scientists Work

Review Questions

1. What is a scientific theory? _____
   _____

2. (a) What are socio-scientific issues? _____
   (b) Give an example of a socio-scientific issue. _____

3. Which of the following questions do you think are appropriate for scientific investigation?

	Yes	No
(a) Who was the best sportsman of the twentieth century?	☐	☐
(b) Can it be too cold to snow?	☐	☐
(c) Is it right to test medicines on animals?	☐	☐
(d) Is it possible to land a satellite on an asteroid?	☐	☐
(e) Should we dump nuclear waste at sea?	☐	☐
(f) Will time travel be possible in the future?	☐	☐
(g) How do ghosts move through walls?	☐	☐
(h) What is spider silk made of?	☐	☐

4. What is a hypothesis? _____
   _____

5. Explain how a hypothesis develops into a theory. _____
   _____

6. Explain the difference between a controlled experiment and an observational experiment.
   _____

Knowledge and Understanding

Case Study BT Young Scientist & Technology Exhibition

Ciara Judge, Sophie Healy-Thow and Émer Hickey from Kinsale Community School, Co. Cork won the BT young scientist competition in 2013. Their project was entitled 'A statistical investigation of the effects of diazotroph bacteria on plant germination.'

Émer and her mum were gardening, and she noticed nodules* on one of their pea plants. She brought the plant into school,

Fig. 1 Winners 2013: Ciara Judge, Sophie Healy-Thow and Émer Hickey

and her teacher told her the nodules contained bacteria. The girls carried out a detailed experiment to investigate if coating the seeds of cereals such as barley, wheat and oats with a certain type of bacteria would affect the speed at which they would germinate and influence the growth of the crops. Their project showed that treating the seeds with the special bacteria reduced the germination time by almost half, and increased the yield of the crops. This project addressed an important issue in the world – food shortages. In many developing countries, crops can fail or not grow enough to provide food for the community. Their project discovered a possible way to deal with this problem.

*Nodules are swellings on the roots of some leguminous plants like peas and clover, which contain bacteria.

Questions
1. What was the initial observation on which this investigation was based?
2. How was the initial observation developed into a testable hypothesis?
3. What strategy did the girls use to test their hypothesis?
4. What other strategies could the girls have used to test their hypothesis?
5. (a) Identify the cause and effect variables in this investigation.
   (b) Which variables were controlled by the investigators?
6. Explain how this investigation may be considered to be a socio-scientific issue.
7. This project was called a 'statistical investigation'. What does this tell you about the way that the results of this experiment were analysed?

Analyse and Interpret

1. The diagram shows a sequence of four drawings representing the formation of a hurricane, starting from the top drawing. This type of representation can be called a model.

   (a) Why do scientists use models?

   (b) There is no description included in this model. Look carefully at the diagrams and use them to write a description of how you think hurricanes are formed.

   (c) How could this model be used to make predictions?

   (d) How could computers be used to improve the value of a model like this?

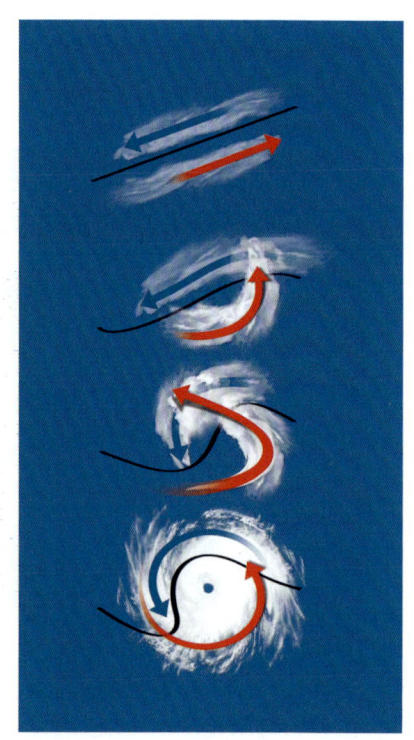

4 Scientific Investigations

Review Questions

Select the correct answers for each of these questions:

1. A scientist bases a hypothesis on:
   (a) Ideas ☐   (b) Observations ☐   (c) Facts ☐   (d) None of these ☐   (e) All of these ☐

2. Scientists test their hypotheses using:
   (a) Books ☐   (b) Discussions ☐   (c) Investigations ☐   (d) Conclusions ☐

3. The information collected from an experiment is called:
   (a) Proof ☐   (b) Conclusion ☐   (c) Method ☐   (d) Data ☐

4. A factor that is changed or measured by a scientist is called:
   (a) Control ☐   (b) Variable ☐   (c) Measurement ☐   (d) Observation ☐

Knowledge and Understanding

1. All experiments should be fair. To ensure a fair experiment how many cause variables should be changed at the same time? Justify your answer.

2. A scientist decides to investigate the effect of temperature on the time it takes for sugar to dissolve in water. Identify the cause variable that they would change and the effect variable that they would measure.

3. Explain the difference between qualitative and quantitative data.

4. Scientists need precise results so that they can draw conclusions. What is meant by precise results?

5. Which of these instruments is more accurate for measuring the volume of a liquid:
   (a) Beaker (b) Flask (c) Graduated cylinder? Justify your answer.

6. (a) Which instrument would be more accurate when measuring the diameter of a small pipe – a Vernier callipers or a ruler?
   (b) Suggest a way that a golfer's accuracy could be measured.

7. Which of these sets of data is more precise? Justify your answer.

| Experiment A | Volume of acid (cm³) | 19.1 | 18.3 | 19.9 |
| Experiment B | Volume of acid (cm³) | 19.2 | 19.4 | 19.3 |

Case Study The strange case of beriberi

Dr Christiaan Eijkman was a Dutch doctor who worked in Indonesia in the 1880s and 1890s. At this time a disease called beriberi was very common. The symptoms of beriberi include weakness and loss of appetite, and victims often died of heart failure. Scientists thought that beriberi may be caused by bacteria. Dr Eijkman investigated the disease. He chose chickens for his experiments on this disease as they were cheap, easy to keep and they develop disease more quickly than humans.

His first hypothesis was that the disease was caused by bacteria. His experiment involved two sets of healthy chickens. One set was injected with bacteria from the blood of people who had died from beriberi. The second set of chickens were not injected. In this experiment all the chickens got sick, including those that had not been injected. Dr Eijkman decided to set up an experiment at a different location as he thought the first location may have been contaminated. As he did this, however, all the chickens got well. He was puzzled as he had done nothing to cure them.

The man who had been in charge of feeding the chickens at the first location had told Dr Eijkman that he had fed the chickens with white rice. A new cook arrived and fed them brown rice. It was then that the chickens had recovered.

Dr Eijkman designed new experiments to test a different variable. He divided the chickens up into different experiment groups:
- He fed one group of sick chickens with white rice.
- He fed one group of sick chickens with brown rice.
- He fed one group of healthy chickens with white rice.
- He fed one group of healthy chickens with brown rice.

His results were that chickens that were fed white rice remained sick or became sick and that chickens fed brown rice became healthy or remained healthy.

Scientific Investigations   4

Dr Eijkman's conclusion was that the brown rice contained a substance that prevented beriberi. Further work by other scientists led to the identification of nutrients such as vitamins in food. In 1926 vitamin B1, thiamine, was discovered. This was found to be the vitamin that prevents beriberi. We now know that the chickens that were fed brown rice were getting vitamin B1. In 1929 Dr Eijkman together with Sir Frederick Hopkins was awarded the Nobel Prize in Physiology or Medicine.

Questions
1. What was the problem that Dr Eijkman identified?
2. What was Dr Eijkman's hypothesis?
3. How did he first test his hypothesis?
4. Did the results of his first experiment support or reject his hypothesis?
5. Suggest the hypothesis that his second experiment tested.
6. How did the work of other scientists build on Dr. Eijkman's conclusion?

5 Communication and Research in Science

Review Questions

1. List four ways that scientists communicate with each other and the public:
   (a) _____ (b) _____ (c) _____ (d) _____
2. Scientists communicate to share ideas. How do scientific ideas become theories?
   _____
   _____
3. How do scientists communicate informally? _____
4. How do scientists communicate formally? _____
5. What is a primary source of information? _____
6. What is a secondary source of information? _____
7. Are the following primary (P) or secondary (S) sources of information?

	P	S
(a) Results from an investigation you carried out.	☐	☐
(b) Video footage of an event.	☐	☐
(c) An article from *Science* magazine.	☐	☐
(d) Information from NASA website.	☐	☐
(e) An interview with a scientist.	☐	☐
(f) An encyclopedia.	☐	☐
(g) A school textbook.	☐	☐
(h) Data collected by a computer program you set up.	☐	☐

8. Give two examples of scientific journals. (a) _____ (b) _____

Knowledge and Understanding

1. What is meant by bias? Why is it important that a source of information does not have bias?
2. Sometimes scientific information presented in the media has been misinterpreted. Why is it important that information in the media is presented accurately?
3. A research project may be broken into three stages. Outline these three stages.
4. How can you check the reliability of a source of information?
5. What must you consider when deciding how to present a project?
6. What information is included when referencing a secondary source?

Case Study Chocolate 'as good for you as exercise'

Research suggests that chocolate is as good for you as exercise. Scientists have found that small amounts of dark chocolate may improve health in a similar way to exercise. The researchers focused on the mitochondria. These are the tiny powerhouses in cells that generate energy. They discovered that a special plant compound found in chocolate appeared to stimulate the same muscle response as vigorous activity.

Dr Moh Malek, who led the study on mice,

Communication and Research in Science 5

said, 'Mitochondria produce energy which is used by the cells in the body. More mitochondria mean more energy is produced and more work can be performed.

'Exercise such as running or cycling is known to increase the number of mitochondria in muscle cells. Our study has found that the plant compound found in chocolate also seems to increase the number of mitochondria.'

Some of this plant compound from cocoa was given to a group of mice twice a day for 15 days. At the same time, another group of mice underwent 30 minutes of treadmill training each day.

Researchers found that mice that were only fed the special plant compound were able to perform athletically to the same level as those running on the treadmill.

The findings were published in the *Journal of Physiology*. The scientists hope their research will lead to better ways of combating muscle wasting in humans.

Dr Malek said, 'At the moment it would be a leap of faith to say the same effects would be seen in humans. But it is something we hope to identify in future studies.'

The Telegraph (adapted)

Questions
1. What are the findings of this research?
2. What evidence do the scientists provide to support the health benefits of chocolate?
3. Do you think the evidence supports the claim in the headline that chocolate is 'as good for you as exercise'?
4. How could the findings of this study be misinterpreted?
5. (a) Where was this research published? (b) Are these types of publications respected?
6. Write an advertisement for a chocolate bar. How could you use the information in this case study to promote the product?

Case Study Early CT scans prevent lung cancer deaths

An American scientist and her team carried out research on early CT scans and lung cancer. CT scans can produce 3-D images of parts of the body. The team investigated the impact of having early CT scans of the lungs on the number of people who died from lung cancer.

In 2006 the scientist published her findings in a respected scientific journal. She reported that her study showed that 80% of lung cancer deaths could be prevented through the widespread use of early CT scans. The detection of cancer at an early stage would mean that the patient would receive treatment earlier. It was later found out that the study was funded by a major tobacco company.

Questions
1. Why do you think a tobacco company would fund this research?
2. Do you think that the way this study was funded would have had an effect on the findings that were *published*?
3. Do you think that private companies should fund scientific research? Explain your answer.

6   Discovery and Invention

Review Questions

1. Make a list of 10 inventions that you use every day.
   1. _____ 2. _____ 3. _____ 4. _____ 5. _____
   6. _____ 7. _____ 8. _____ 9. _____ 10. _____

2. What do you consider the most important invention? _____

3. Describe what life would be like without this invention. _____
   _____
   _____

Knowledge and Understanding

1. Below are pictures of inventions and discoveries.
   (a) Suggest a reason why each was invented.
   (b) Consider what life would be like without it.
   (c) What impact has it had on society?

A. Electric toaster

B. Plastic

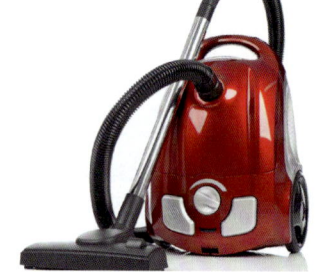

C. Vacuum cleaner

D. Television

E. Soap

F. Zip

Discovery and Invention 6

G. Diesel lawnmower

H. Electric kettle

I. Toilet

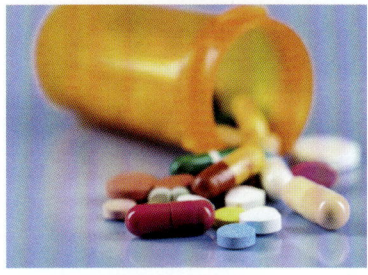
J. Antibiotics

K. Car

L. Fibre optic cables

M. Smart phone

N. Wheel

O. Internet

P. Ring pull tin can

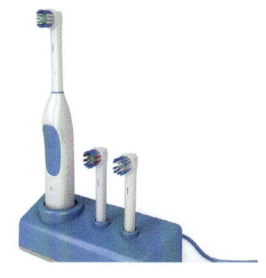
Q. Electric toothbrush

R. Aeroplane

2. The table shows a list of important scientific discoveries and inventions. Order them according to how important you think they are to society, for example, 1 for the most important, 13 for the least important. Explain your choice of numbers 1 and 13.

Invention		No.
A	Electricity	_____.
B	Disinfectant	_____.
C	Radioactive elements	_____.
D	The wheel	_____.
E	The steam engine	_____.
F	The internet	_____.
G	Structure of DNA	_____.
H	Vaccinations	_____.
I	Antibiotics	_____.
J	Radio	_____.
K	Facebook	_____.
L	iPhone	_____.
M	Cloning	_____.

7 Cell Structure and Function

Review Questions

1. Give an example of a living thing that is composed of only one cell.
   _____

2. Give an example of a living thing that is made up of millions of cells.
   _____

3. Examine the diagram of the microscope and mark in the following:
   (a) V – illuminates the specimen
   (b) W – look through this to see the specimen
   (c) X – the slide is placed here
   (d) Y – magnifies the specimen
   (e) Z – an image at high magnification can be focused with this

4. List two important procedures when preparing a slide for examination. Explain why they are important.
   (a) _____
   _____
   (b) _____
   _____

5. If an eyepiece has a magnification of ×10 and an objective lens has a magnification of ×10, what is the total magnification of the two lenses? _____

6. Plant and animal cells have many common structures. However, plant cells also contain structures that are not present in an animal cell.
   Arrange the following into the correct column in the table below:
   (a) Cell membrane, (b) Chloroplast, (c) Nucleus, (d) Cytoplasm, (e) Large vacuole, (f) Cell wall, (g) Mitochondria

In plant and animal cells	Only in plant cells

7. Why is a cell membrane said to be semi-permeable? Why is this important to the cell?
   _____
   _____

8. A group of cells working together is called a tissue. List two tissues in the human body.
   (a) _____ (b) _____

9. Organs are groups of tissues working together. Give two examples of organs in the human body and name the systems they are part of.
   (a) Organ: _____ System: _____
   (b) Organ: _____ System: _____

10. Where does photosynthesis take place in a plant cell? _____
11. What feature of a muscle cell allows movement in an animal? _____
12. How is the structure of a sperm cell related to its function? _____
13. How is the structure of a red blood cell related to its function of carrying oxygen? _____
    _____
14. Which plant system is above ground? _____
15. Which plant system is below ground? _____

Knowledge and Understanding

1. Draw a diagram of a plant cell and an animal cell. Insert the labels A–G in your diagram:
   A – Some substances are allowed to travel through this structure.
   B – Gives the cell structure and support
   C – Controls the cell's activities
   D – Respiration occurs here
   E – Photosynthesis occurs here
   F – Water and dissolved substances are temporarily stored here
   G – Contains the cell's genetic information in the form of DNA

2. The plant cells in Fig. 1 contain a lot of chloroplasts. Suggest where these cells may be found in a plant and name the function they carry out.

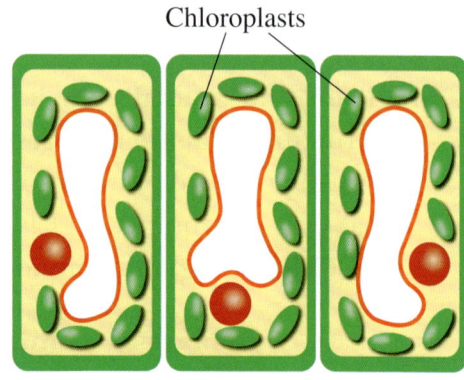

Fig. 1

3. Fig. 2 shows a type of cell that lines the airways in animals. It contains little hairs on its surface. What do you think the function of these little hairs could be? Give an explanation for your answer.

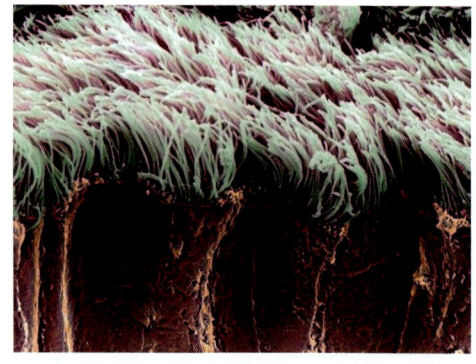

Fig. 2

Cell Structure and Function 7

4. Draw a flow chart to show how the following terms are related: tissue, system, cell, organ, organism.

Analyse and Interpret

Mitochondria are structures in a cell where respiration takes place. Respiration produces energy for the cell. Analyse this chart and answer the questions which follow.

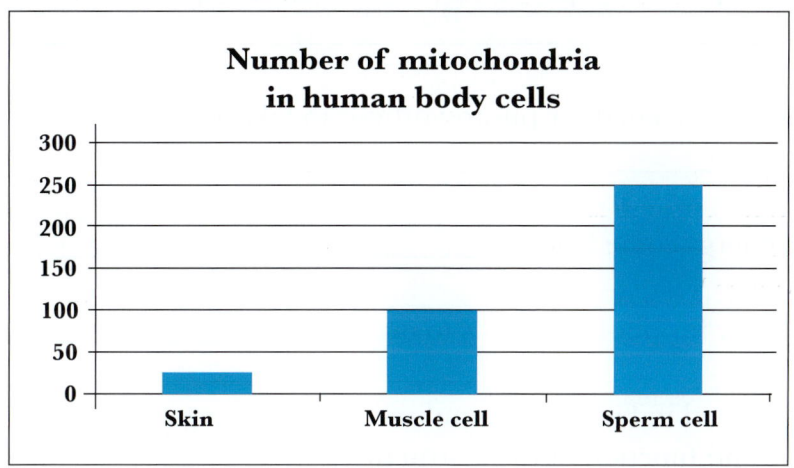

(a) Why do you think skin cells have the least number of mitochondria?
(b) Why do you think muscle cells need more mitochondria than skin cells?
(c) Why do you think sperm cells have more than twice the number of mitochondria that muscle cells have?
(d) If a person carried out regular aerobic exercise what would you expect to happen to the numbers of mitochondria in their muscle cells?
(e) If a person had to stay in bed due to illness, what would you expect to happen to the numbers of mitochondria in their muscle cells?

8 Cell Processes
Photosynthesis and Respiration

Review Questions

1. In which part of the plant does photosynthesis mainly take place?
   _____

2. What type of energy is needed for photosynthesis to take place?
   _____

3. Where does this energy come from? _____

4. What gas is necessary for photosynthesis to occur? _____

5. The structures pictured in Fig. 1 are found on the undersurface of a leaf. What is the name and function of these structures? _____
   _____
   _____

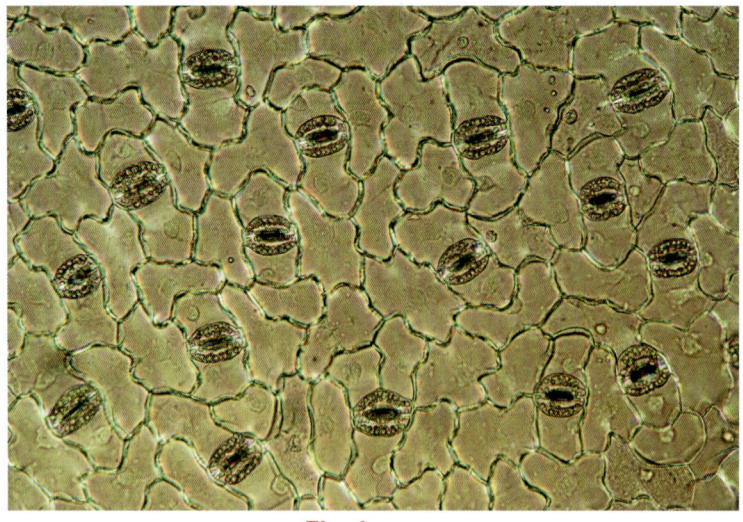

Fig. 1

6. Describe how a leaf is specially adapted for photosynthesis.
   _____
   _____
   _____

7. Use the words below to write out the equation for photosynthesis.

   chlorophyll   water   oxygen   carbon dioxide   light   glucose

   _____ + _____ → _____ + _____

Cell Processes: Photosynthesis and Respiration   8

8. What food molecule is produced by a plant during photosynthesis? _____

9. What type of tissue transports food around the plant? _____

10. In what form is food stored in a plant? _____

11. Give an example of a plant that stores food in its root. _____

12. List two factors that affect the rate of photosynthesis in a plant.
    (i) _____
    (ii) _____

13. Life could not exist on Earth without green plants.
    Give as many reasons as you can to support this statement.
    _____
    _____
    _____

14. Where does respiration occur in a cell? _____

15. What type of respiration requires oxygen? _____

16. Write out the word equation for this type of respiration.
    _____

17. What type of respiration does not require oxygen? _____

18. Name one type of microorganism that can produce energy by anaerobic respiration.
    _____

19. Why do you think muscle cells have more mitochondria than fat cells?
    _____

20. Which gas is produced as a waste product of respiration? _____

21. How does a mammal remove this gas from its body? _____

22. Under what circumstances does anaerobic respiration sometimes occur in the muscles of an animal? _____
    _____

23. What substance causes the burning sensation in muscles after exercise?
    _____

24. Why do humans breathe faster when they exercise?
    _____
    _____

25

Analyse and Interpret

A student carried out an experiment to investigate the effect of distance from a lamp on the rate of photosynthesis in the pond weed, Elodea.

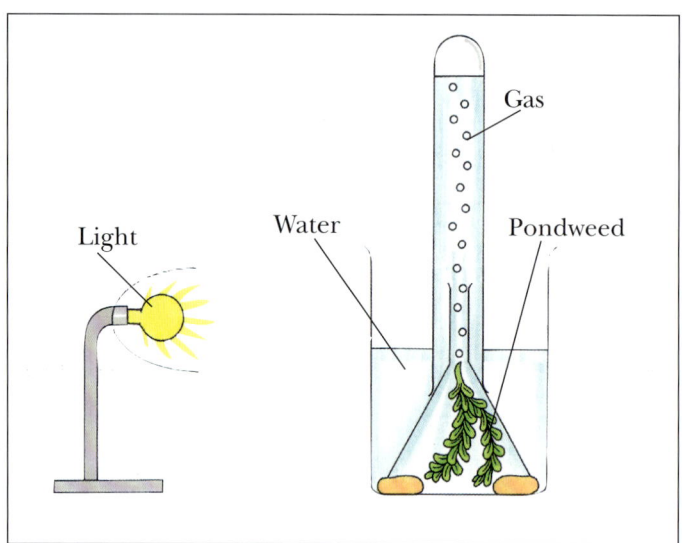

A 100 watt bulb was used in the experiment. The plant was kept at a constant temperature of 25°C and had sufficient carbon dioxide. The bulb was placed at 1.0 m, 0.75 m, 0.5 m, 0.25 m and 0.1 m away from the plant.

The rate of photosynthesis was measured by counting the number of bubbles coming out of the Elodea per minute for three minutes at each distance. An average was then taken of the three readings.
The following results were obtained.

Distance of lamp from Elodea	Average number of bubbles produced per minute
1.0 m	10
0.75 m	20
0.5 m	25
0.25 m	30
0.1 m	30

1. What is the cause variable in this experiment?
2. What is the effect variable in this experiment?
3. What factors did the student keep constant? Why did he/she do this?
4. Suggest how the temperature could be maintained at 25°C.
5. What gas is contained in the bubbles produced by Elodea?
6. Do you think that counting the number of bubbles produced by Elodea is a good way to measure the rate of photosynthesis? Explain your answer.
7. Why did the student calculate an average result for three minutes?
8. Why is it important that the plant had sufficient carbon dioxide?

Cell Processes: Photosynthesis and Respiration   8

9. Using the section of blank graph paper below, draw a graph to illustrate the results obtained.

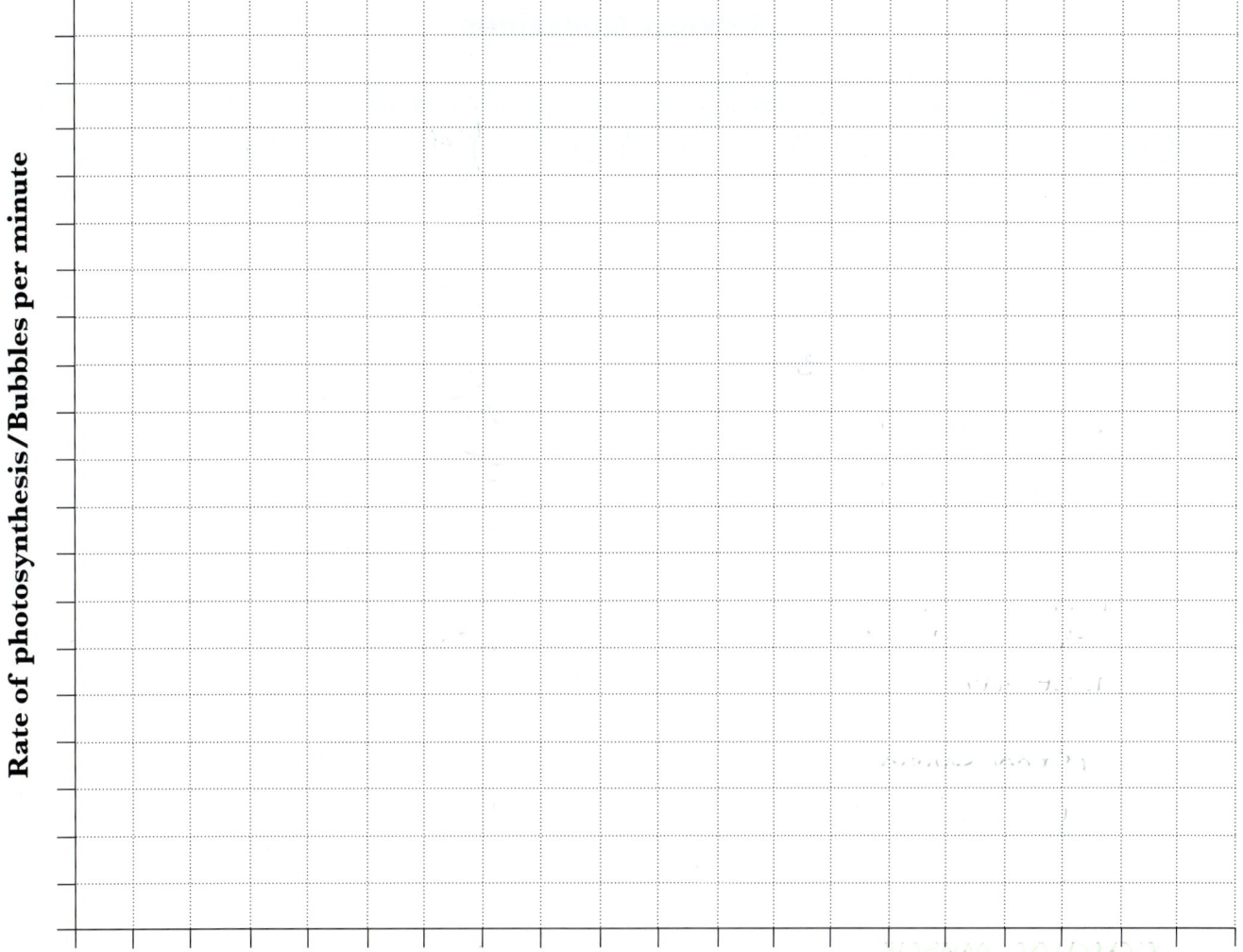

Distance from lamp vs Rate of photosynthesis in Elodea

Rate of photosynthesis/Bubbles per minute

Distance from lamp

10. What conclusion do you think the student will come to about the relationship between the distance from the lamp and the rate of photosynthesis?

11. Suggest a reason why the rate of photosynthesis is the same when the lamp is 0.25 m and 0.1 m away from the Elodea.

9 The Circulatory System

Review Questions

1. What is the approximate (a) size and (b) location of the heart?
   (a) of a clenched fist (b) to the left of your chest area.

2. Label this diagram of the heart.

   A = Aorta
   B = pulmonary artery
   C = right atrium
   D = right ventricle
   E = septum
   F = left ventricle
   G = left atrium
   H = vena cava
   I = pulmonary vein

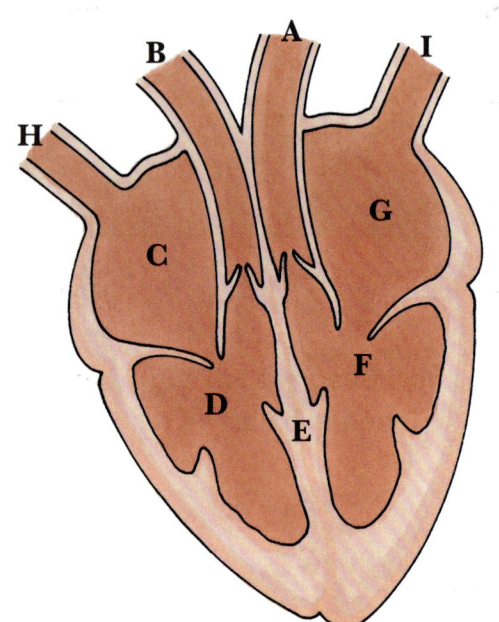

3. What type of muscle is the heart made of?
   Cardiac muscle

4. Name the blood vessel that supplies the heart muscle with blood.
   ~~veins~~ aortas?

5. What type of blood vessel carries blood away from the heart?
   ~~artery~~ pulmonary artery

6. What type of blood vessel carries blood to the heart?
   ~~veins~~ vena cava

7. Fill in the following table.

Vessel	Carries	From	To
Vena cava	Deoxygenated blood	Body	Heart
Pulmonary artery	deoxygenated blood	Heart	lungs
Pulmonary vein	oxygenated blood	lungs	left atria
Aorta	oxygenated blood	Heart	body

28

The Circulatory System   9

8. How is the structure of an artery suited to its function?
It has thick walls and has no valves because of pressure.

9. What structures prevent blood from flowing backwards in a vein?
Valves

10. Why do arteries not need these structures?
They have very high pressure so theres no chance.

11. (a) How thick are the walls of a capillary? Very thin
(b) What importance does this have for the transport of substances around the body?
to allow substances to easily come into the cells.

12. What are the two main components of blood?
plasma and red blood cells

13. Match the blood cells A–C with the correct function 1–3.
  A. Red blood cell — 2. Carries oxygen
  B. White blood cell — 3. Defends against disease
  C. Platelet — 1. Clots the blood

14. List two functions of plasma.
(a) transports substances around the body
(b) being a solvent

15. Draw arrows on the diagram to illustrate the flow of blood through the heart.

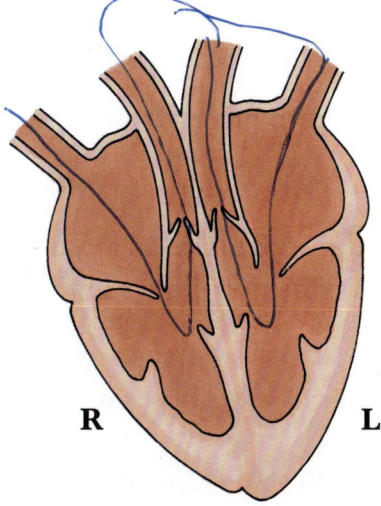

16. Why does the left side of the heart have a thicker wall than the right?
because it has to pump blood into all parts of the body making it stronger.

17. The diagram to the right shows a model of the system which is used to circulate blood around the body.

(a) Name the organ which is responsible for pumping blood around the body.

heart

(b) Arrows are drawn in the diagram to indicate the direction in which blood flows in that part of the system. Draw arrows on the diagram to indicate the direction in which blood flows in other parts of the system.

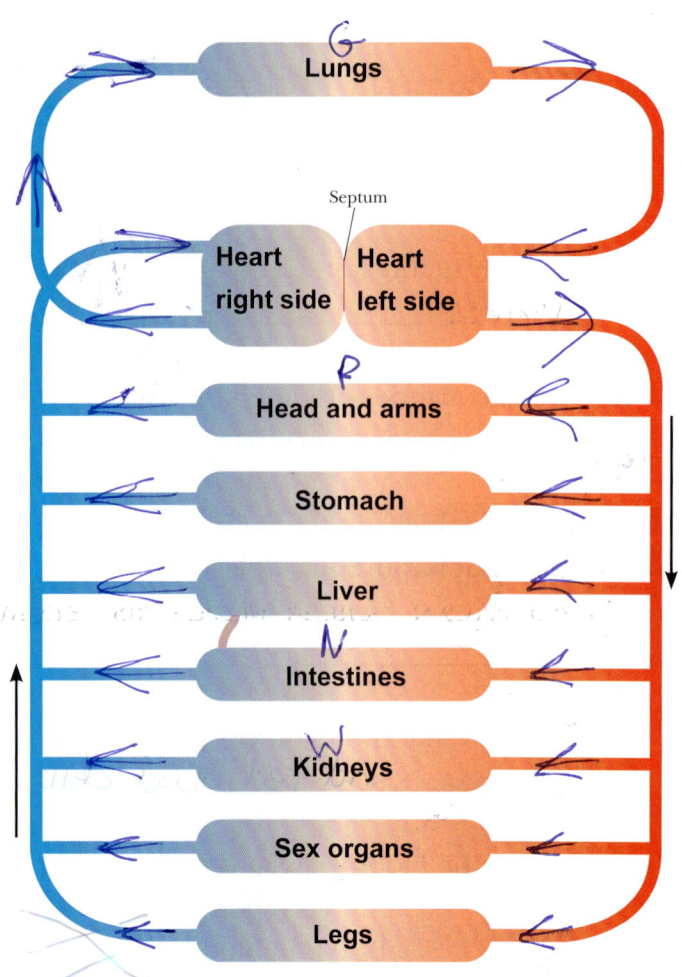

(c) Mark with the letter G a place in the system where the blood gains oxygen.

(d) Mark with the letter L a place in the system where the blood loses oxygen.

(e) Mark with the letter W a place in the system where waste is removed from the blood.

(f) Mark with the letter N a place in the system where the blood absorbs nutrients.

(g) Describe one function of the circulatory system which does not involve the transport of substances around the body. to remove waste from cells and organs

(h) The body needs nutrients and oxygen for respiration. Describe what happens during respiration and why this process is important for living things. The cells take in oxygen and release carbon dioxide.

(i) Mark with the letter P a place in the system where a person's pulse could be measured.

(j) Explain why a person's pulse might increase while they are exercising. because their heartrate is up.

(k) Name one lifestyle choice that could cause a person's resting pulse to increase over time.
a lot of stress

The Circulatory System 9

Knowledge and Understanding

1. The circulation of blood in mammals is called double circulation. Where do each of the two circuits go? *the two circuits go to two different places in the body at the same time.*

2. Where can you detect a pulse in the human body? Why can you detect it here? *At the wrist and neck*

3. List the lifestyle factors that help to maintain a healthy heart. *exercise, have a healthy weight, eat well, avoid alcohol and smoking and reduce stress.*

4. How can a diet high in animal fats affect the circulatory system? *it builds up and leads to atherosclerosis.*

5. EPO, or erythropoietin, is an illegal drug used to improve performance in athletes. It works by increasing the amount of red blood cells in the blood. Why do you think this drug improves an athlete's performance? Why do you think it is illegal to use EPO? *to strengthen and improve their muscles for a short period of time. I think its because it gives the athletes to much of a boost, which is unfair to the other athletes.*

6. Rob Heffernan is an Irish race walker. He won gold in the 50 km walk at the 2013 World Athletics Championships. Rob and many other athletes train at high altitudes or use special chambers that mimic the conditions at high altitudes. The air at a higher altitude has lower levels of oxygen.

    How do you think this form of training will improve an athlete's performance in an event at a lower altitude? *I think because he trained at a higher altitude, his lungs and heart grew stronger and got used to the lack of oxygen in the*

10 Food and the Digestive System

Review Questions

1. The diagram shows the human digestive system.

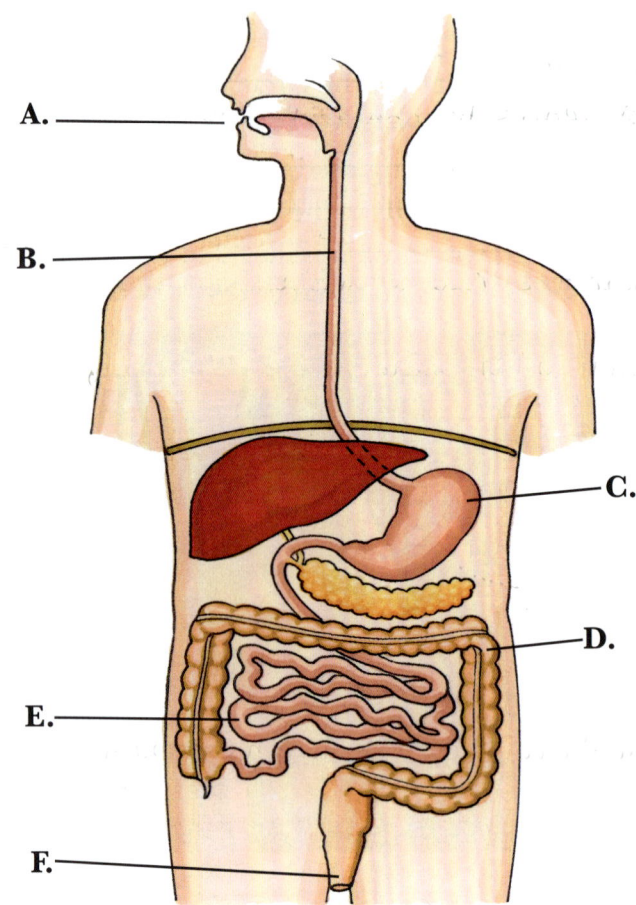

Read the statements 1–6 and match them with the labels A–F.
1. Food is fully digested and absorbed here.   1 = _____
2. Waste is passed out from here.   2 = _____
3. Food is mixed with acid and enzymes and churned here.   3 = _____
4. Food is pushed down into the stomach here.   4 = _____
5. Food is physically digested here and mixed with saliva.   5 = _____
6. Water is absorbed here.   6 = _____

2. Name two organs associated with the digestive system and outline their role.
   (a) _____
   (b) _____

3. List the five stages of nutrition. (a) _____ (b) _____
   (c) _____ (d) _____ (e) _____

4. Where does physical digestion occur? _____

Food and the Digestive System — 10

5. Where does chemical digestion occur? _____
   _____

6. (a) Which type of tooth is used for tearing? _____
   (b) How does the shape of this type of tooth suit its function? _____
   _____

Knowledge and Understanding

1. A stomach ulcer is a condition in which the lining of the stomach becomes irritated and can even bleed or develop a hole. Using your understanding of the structure of the stomach and digestion suggest a reason why the stomach lining may become irritated.

2. 'The small intestine is six metres long, however the inner lining of it is much longer.' Do you think this statement is true? Explain your answer.

3. How does the structure of the small intestine relate to its function in digestion and absorption?

4. How do bile and pancreatic juice enter the small intestine?

5. What role do bile and pancreatic juice play in digestion?

6. What is the main role of the large intestine?

7. How do the bacteria in the large intestine affect human health?

8. Explain the importance of fibre in the diet and list three foods that are a good source of fibre.

9. There are three systems that work together to ensure the energy in food is released in every cell of the human body by respiration. In the table below one system has been completed. Give the name and describe the function of the other two systems.

System	Function
The circulatory system	Transports food and oxygen to every cell in the body for respiration and removes waste products such as carbon dioxide.

10. Athletes, particularly long distance runners, eat a lot of carbohydrates before a race. They also eat special high sugar gels during the race. Why do you think athletes have this sort of diet?

11. Coeliac disease is a condition that affects the small intestine. A person with coeliac disease cannot tolerate gluten which is found in wheat, barley and rye. Gluten flattens and damages the villi in the small intestine leaving them unable to function properly.
Using your knowledge of the digestive system, how would damaging the villi in the small intestine affect a person?

12. A person suffering from a throat infection may be treated with antibiotics which kill bacteria. How could antibiotics affect the digestive system?

Case Study The war on sugar, Ireland's changing taste

Irish people today are eating a much different diet than their grandparents did.
 We haven't only accumulated more diverse food options; we've accumulated more weight. Data from the Cork Open Research Archive shows that the average weight of 14-year-old boys in 2002 was 65% greater than in 1948. Similarly 14-year-old girls' weight also increased, by 48%. According to the report 'a substantial proportion of the weight' increase is seen between the 1970s and 2002.

Helen O'Callaghan, *Irish Examiner*

Fig. 1 Irish people now eat more sugar than previous generations

Questions
1. What type of foods do you think your grandparents and great grandparents would have eaten every day?
2. What do you think are the main differences between the average diet in the 1940s and today?
3. Why do you think Irish boys and girls are much heavier now than boys and girls of the same age in 1948?
4. Obese children are more likely to develop health problems later in life. List some of these health problems.
5. Identify the healthy and unhealthy aspects of your diet. How could you improve your diet to make it healthier?

Food and the Digestive System — 10

Analyse and Interpret

1. A group of students carried out an experiment to investigate the effect of temperature on enzyme activity. They tested the effectiveness of the enzyme, salivary amylase, at three different temperatures: 22°C, 37°C and 50°C

   The following table shows the results of the investigation. Effectiveness was measured by the % of maltose formed from the starch solution.

Time (hours)	% of maltose formed from starch solution		
	Temp 22°C	Temp 37°C	Temp 50°C
0.0	0	0	0
0.5	0	2	0
1.0	8	12	4
1.5	20	36	10
2.0	40	66	16
2.5	60	78	22
3.0	70	94	28

   (a) What is an enzyme?
   (b) Draw a single graph to compare the results obtained at each temperature.
   (c) Describe the effects of the different temperatures on the action of salivary amylase.

11 The Respiratory System

Review Questions

1. Label this diagram of the respiratory system
   A. _____
   B. _____
   C. _____
   D. _____
   E. _____
   F. _____
   G. _____

2. On the diagram:
   (a) Mark **W** in a position where rings of cartilage are found.
   (b) Mark **X** where gas exchange occurs.
   (c) Mark **Y** where muscles contract and relax to cause inhalation and exhalation.
   (d) Mark **Z** where sound is generated.

3. What structures prevent dust from entering the bronchioles and alveoli?
   _____
   _____

4. How does the structure of the alveoli maximise gas exchange?
   _____

5. How is oxygen carried in the blood? _____

6. How is carbon dioxide carried in the blood? _____

7. Which process in cells uses oxygen and produces carbon dioxide? _____

8. Which systems are involved in supplying the materials necessary for respiration?
   _____

The Respiratory System 11

Knowledge and Understanding

1. The table shows the composition of inhaled and exhaled air.

Gas	% Volume	
	Inhaled air	Exhaled air
Oxygen	21	16
Carbon dioxide	0.04	4
Nitrogen	79	79
Water vapour	Varies	Saturated

   (a) Explain the difference in oxygen content of inhaled and exhaled air.
   (b) Explain the difference in carbon dioxide content in inhaled and exhaled air.
   (c) Why does the nitrogen content remain the same?
   (d) Why does the water content of inhaled air vary?
   (e) Why is exhaled air saturated with water vapour?
   (f) How could you prove that exhaled air contains more carbon dioxide than inhaled air?

2. What is the advantage of the heart being near the lungs?

3. The following are a list of disorders that affect the respiratory system. How would each disorder affect the proper function of the respiratory system?
   (a) Pneumonia: the alveoli fill with thick fluid.
   (b) Asthma: the airways are inflamed and become narrower.
   (c) Emphysema: alveoli burst and fuse into enlarged air spaces.

4. Outline the symptoms of an inherited disorder that affects the respiratory system.

5. What effect does long-term smoking have on lung tissue?

Analyse and Interpret

1. The graph shows the effect of exercise on the rate of breathing of student A and student B. Both students are the same age and gender. Student A is a member of the school football and basketball teams, trains two evenings per week and walks to and from school every day. Student B is not a member of any sports team and gets a lift to school every day. Analyse the graph and answer the questions that follow.

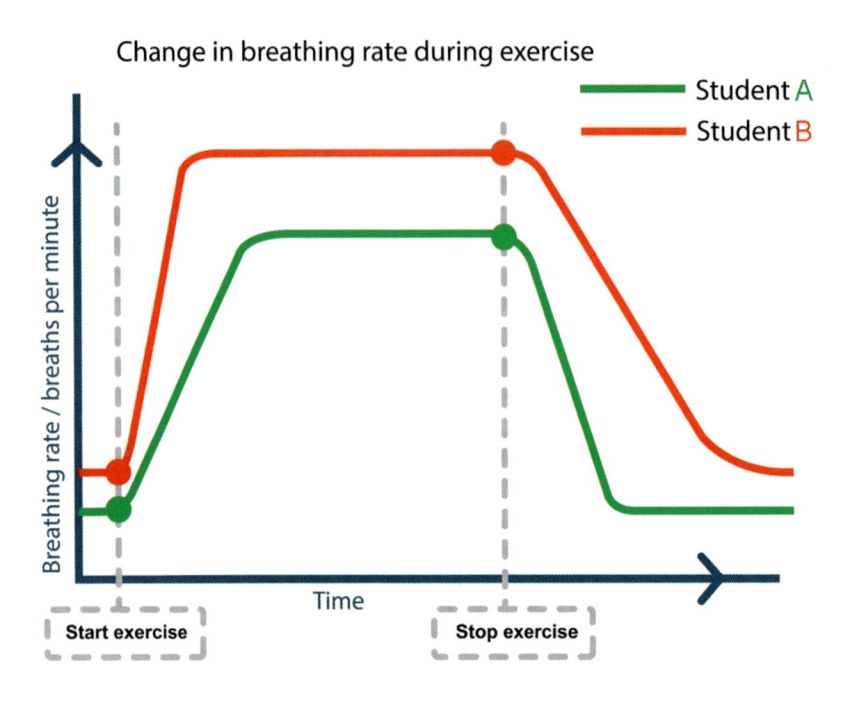

Fig. 1 Changes in breathing rate

(a) Which student has the lower resting breathing rate?

(b) Which student had the most rapid increase in breathing rate after exercise began?

(c) Which student had the lowest breathing rate when exercise had stopped?

(d) Which student recovered more quickly after exercise? Why do you think they recovered more quickly?

(e) In your opinion which student is the fittest? Support your answer.

(f) Copy this graph into your copybook. Using different colours draw a graph to represent the heart rates of student A and student B.

12 Reproduction & Genetics

Review Questions

1. What are the two types of reproduction? (i) _____
   (ii) _____
2. Which type of reproduction involves only one parent?
   _____
3. Which type of reproduction requires two parents?
   _____
4. What is a gamete? _____
5. What is a zygote? _____
6. Describe what happens during fertilisation.
   _____
7. Distinguish between the terms <u>unicellular</u> and <u>multicellular</u>.
   _____
8. Indicate the following on Fig. 1: Cell membrane, Nucleus, Chromosomes.

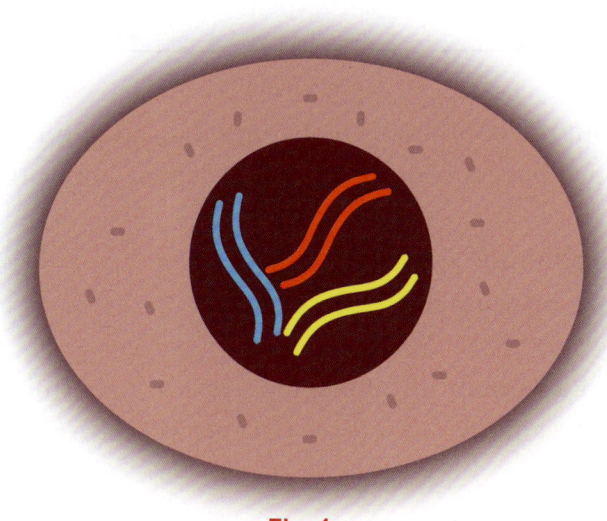

Fig. 1

Fig. 2

9. Fig. 2 represents a pair of chromosomes. What name is given to the coloured sections indicated on the chromosomes? _____

10. What substance are chromosomes made of? _____

Knowledge and Understanding

1. Children that have the same parents often look similar to each other but are never exactly the same. Explain why this is the case.
2. Children often look quite like both of their parents but are never exactly the same as either. Explain why.
3. Genes normally occur in pairs. In humans the gene for brown hair (B) is dominant over the gene for blonde hair (b).

   (a) What term is used to describe a gene which is not dominant?

   (b) What colour hair would a child have if she was born with the following pairs of genes:

   (i) BB

   (ii) Bb

   (iii) bb

   (c) What genes does a child have if he is born with blond hair?

   (d) If a man with blond hair and a woman with brown hair (mixed genes) have a baby, we can use a punnett square to work out what colour the child's hair is likely to be: 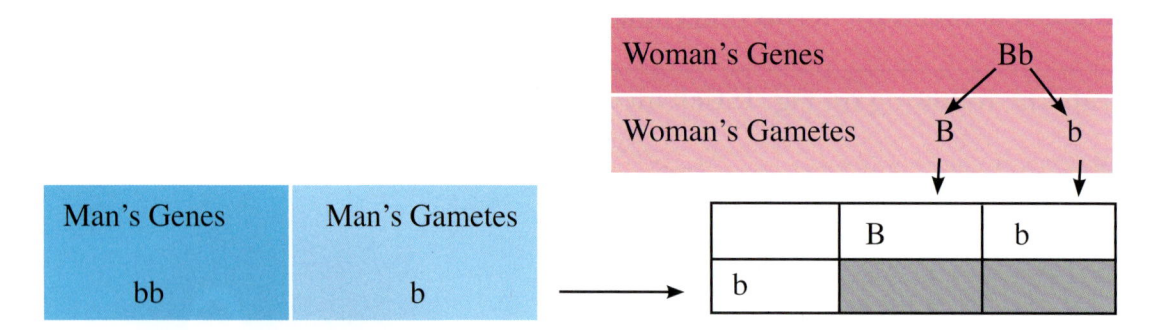

   (i) Complete the punnett square by working out the combination of genes in each of the two grey boxes above. Each box should have two letters representing the pair of genes that the baby could inherit.

   (ii) What are the chances that the baby will have blonde hair?

   (iii) What are the chances that the baby will have brown hair?

4. The punnett square below represents a man and a woman who both have brown hair (mixed genes). Complete the punnett square. What are the chances that these parents will have a child with blond hair?

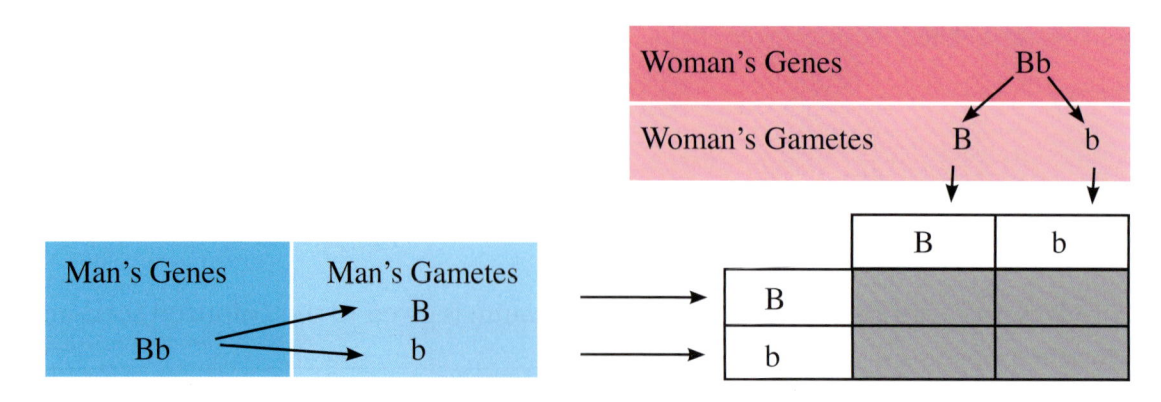

5. A brown-haired man (with two dominant genes) and a blonde-haired woman have a baby. Use a punnett square to find out what the chances are that the baby will have brown hair.

Reproduction & Genetics 12

Analyse and Interpret

1. For each characteristic listed in the table below state whether you think it is mainly affected by genetic factors, environmental factors or both.

	Genetic	Environmental	Both
(a) Number of fingers			
(b) Sporting ability			
(c) Shape of nose			
(d) Intelligence			
(e) Speaking a language			
(f) Eye colour			
(g) Skin colour			
(h) Height			

2. A class of 24 students were lined up in order of height. Their heights were measured and recorded. A list of the results is shown below:

Height of Students (cm)		
147	161	167
153	161	168
154	162	169
154	164	170
155	164	172
156	164	173
157	165	173
160	167	179

(a) What was the height of the smallest student?
(b) What was the height of the tallest student?
(c) What is the height range of the students in this class?
(d) What was the average height of students in the class?
(e) A summary table of these results is shown below. Complete the table by recording the number of students in each height range.

Summary Table

Height Range (cm)	Number of Students	Height Range (cm)	Number of Students
140 – 144		165 – 169	
145 – 149		170 – 174	
150 – 154		175 – 179	
155 – 159		180 – 184	
160 – 164			

(f) Use the data in your completed summary table to draw a histogram.

(g) What does the histogram tell you about the variation of height in the class?
_____

(h) Carry out a similar survey of the pupils in your own class. How do the results compare with this example? _____

3. The photograph below shows some Cuban land snails (Polymitapicta).
   (a) In what ways do you think these snails differ from each other?
   (b) How do you think scientists analyse the patterns of variation within this species of snail?
   (c) Why is variation important for the long-term survival of a species?

13 Reproduction in Humans

Review Questions

1. What term is used to describe sex cells?
   _____

2. What is the male sex cell called?
   _____

3. What is the female sex cell called?
   _____

4. What is the process that occurs when male and female gametes fuse?
   _____

5. What is the function of the sperm duct?
   _____

6. What is meant by ovulation?
   _____

7. What is the function of the fallopian tubes?
   _____

8. Where in the female reproductive system does fertilisation occur?
   _____

9. The diagram in Fig. 1 is of the male reproductive system.
   Give the role of each of the parts labelled A, B and C.
   A. _____
   B. _____
   C. _____

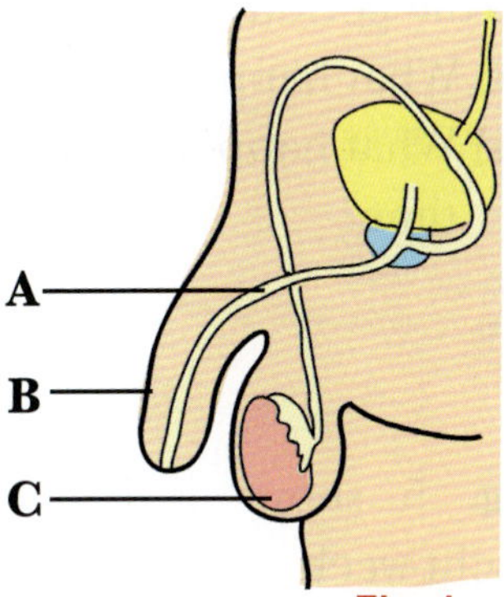

   Fig. 1

10. Fig. 2 represents the 28 days of a typical menstrual cycle.
    (a) What stage of the cycle is represented by A?
    _____

    (b) Describe the changes that occur in the uterus during B.
    _____

    (c) What significant event occurs during C?
    _____

    (d) What may happen during D?
    _____

    (e) What name is given to the period of time represented
        by E? _____
    (f) What happens to the menstrual cycle when a woman
        becomes pregnant? _____

    Fig. 2

    (g) What term is used to describe the time when a woman's menstrual cycle stops completely?
    _____

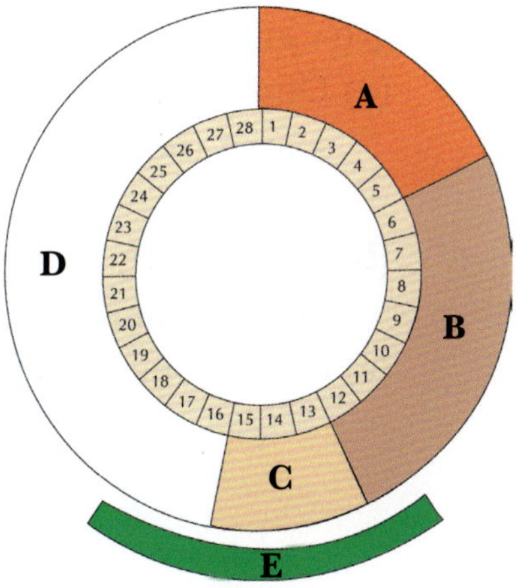

43

11. Fig. 3 shows a baby developing in the uterus. The baby is surrounded by fluid.

(a) What is the fluid called?
_____
_____

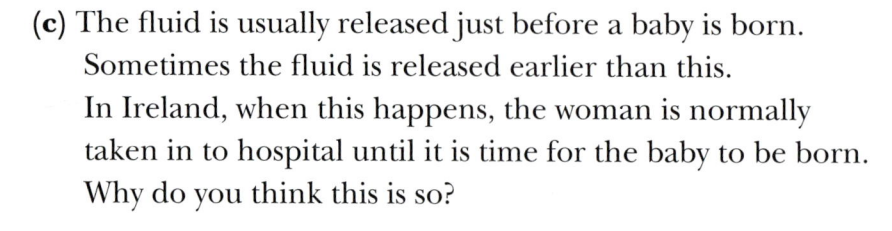

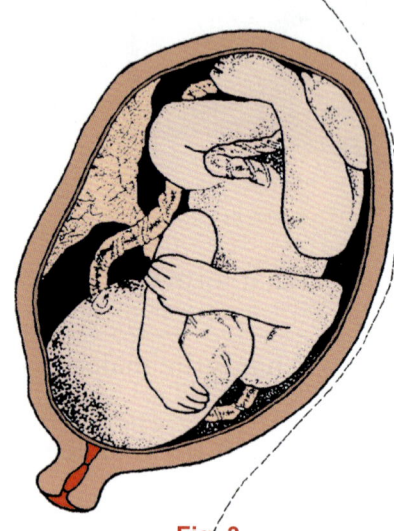

(b) What is the function of the fluid?
_____
_____

(c) The fluid is usually released just before a baby is born. Sometimes the fluid is released earlier than this. In Ireland, when this happens, the woman is normally taken in to hospital until it is time for the baby to be born. Why do you think this is so?
_____
_____

(d) What is the function of the placenta? _____

(e) How is the baby connected to the placenta? _____

Fig. 3

Knowledge and Understanding

1. Fig. 4 shows the female reproductive system during the fertile period of the menstrual cycle.

(a) What happens in the ovary during this time?

(b) What happens to the lining of the uterus during this time?

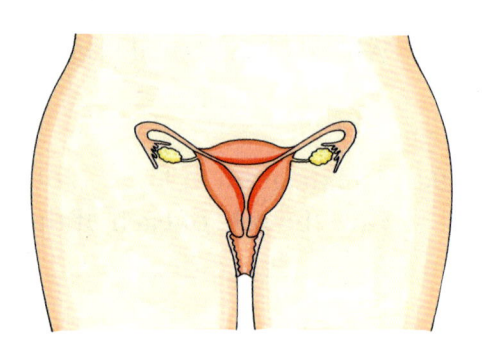

Fig. 4

2. Fig. 5 shows a female reproductive system with an eight-week embryo (foetus) which is clearly recognisable as human. The organs of the foetus are formed and will grow and mature for the next seven months.

(a) Using an arrow and the label S, mark where the semen (liquid containing sperm) was released into the female.

(b) Mark clearly on your diagram, using an arrow and the label F, where fertilisation took place.

(c) Explain the term fertilisation.

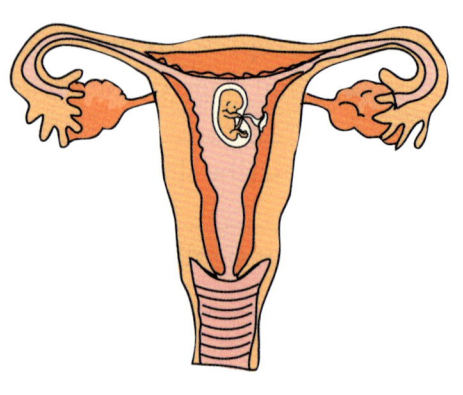

Fig. 5

Reproduction in Humans — 13

3. Read the following article and answer the questions below.

Case Study: IVF in Ireland

In vitro fertilisation (IVF) is the process by which eggs are removed from a woman's ovaries and mixed with sperm in a laboratory dish. Fertilisation takes place in this dish, and the tiny embryos which form are then transferred into the woman's uterus.

Fig. 6 Sperm and eggs are mixed in a Petri dish.

IVF is now a booming industry in Ireland with approximately 26 fertility clinics offering a range of fertility treatments including IVF. IVF uses drugs which stimulate the ovaries to produce more than eight eggs which will then be fertilised in the laboratory. A standard IVF treatment can cost anything from €3,800 to €7,000 and has a 31% success rate. IVF specialists predict that the current rate of one in six couples who are experiencing difficulties conceiving naturally will rise to one in four within the decade.

It is claimed that the reason for this rise has to do with changes in lifestyle. Many couples are delaying having children, preferring to rear a family only after establishing a stable relationship and financial security. There is also a growing number of late and second marriages.

IVF treatment is not without its risks. The drugs used to stimulate the ovaries can cause complications which can be severe.

Some people believe that state funding is required to radically tackle the rise in infertility. They think we should be looking at preventing fertility problems by promoting healthy diet and exercise for children in secondary school.

Irish Independent (adapted)

Questions
(a) Identify and discuss one medical issue related to IVF.
(b) Identify and discuss one ethical issue related to IVF.
(c) Identify and discuss one societal issue related to IVF.
(d) Identify two ways in which fertility problems can be prevented from occurring.

14 Evolution

Review Questions

1. Who first proposed the theory of Evolution by Natural Selection? _____

2. What is meant by variation in a species? _____

3. What is meant by saying that a characteristic is inheritable? _____

4. In relation to evolution what is meant by adaptation? _____

5. Give an example of an adaptation in (a) an animal (b) a plant.
   (a) _____
   (b) _____

6. In relation to living things what is meant by diversity? _____

7. What is a niche? _____

8. Is the amount of body muscle in a person influenced mainly by genetic factors or environmental factors or both? _____

9. Do you think that muscle size is inheritable? _____

10. Do body builders always have children with big muscles? _____

11. Why must variation in a trait be present in order for natural selection to occur? _____

Evolution 14

Knowledge and Understanding

1. South Georgia is an island in the Antarctic Ocean. It is home to both gentoo and macaroni penguins. Macaroni penguins feed only on shrimp-like creatures called krill. They hunt during the night and during the day. Gentoo penguins feed on fish as well as krill. They only feed during the day.

Fig. 1 Macaroni penguins

Fig. 2 Gentoo penguin

(a) Do gentoo and macaroni penguins have the same habitat?
(b) Do gentoo and macaroni penguins have the same diet?
(c) Do gentoo and macaroni penguins occupy the same niche?
(d) Do you think there is competition between gentoo and macaroni penguins?

Krill are found in shallow waters during the night but they hide in deep water during the day.

(e) Which species of penguin would you expect to be better at diving?
(f) How would you expect a penguin to be adapted for diving in deep waters?

According to the theory of evolution by natural selection gentoo and macaroni penguins share a common ancestor which was also a penguin.

(g) Explain how these two separate species of penguin may have evolved from a common ancestor.
(h) What do you think the niche of the common ancestor may have been?
(i) What do you think the common ancestor may have looked like?

2. In 1831 Charles Darwin set sail on board *HMS Beagle*, a British Navy survey ship. In 1835 the ship reached the Galapagos Islands. On the Galapagos Islands Darwin discovered a number of animals that were not found any where else in the world. Two of these animals were the Galapagos marine iguana and the flightless cormorant. The marine iguana is similar to iguanas found elsewhere except that it is the only species of iguana that finds its food in the sea. The marine iguana has slightly webbed toes and its tail is flatter than other iguanas. It can swim and hold its breath for a long time.

Fig. 3 The Galapagos marine iguana.

The flightless cormorant is similar to cormorants found elsewhere except that it cannot fly. However, its little wings allow it to dive more easily than other birds.

In 1859 Darwin published his famous book *On the Origin of Species*. How do you think that what he observed on the Galapagos Islands helped him to form his theory of evolution by natural selection?

Fig. 4 The flightless cormorant.

15 Human Health

Review Questions

1. How does the World Health Organisation define health? _____
   _____

2. What are micro-organisms? _____

3. (a) Name the three types of micro-organisms A, B and C shown in the diagram below.
   A. _____ B. _____ C. _____

   (b) List two illnesses caused by type A micro-organism.
   (i) _____ (ii) _____

   (c) List three illnesses caused by type B micro-organism.
   (i) _____ (ii) _____ (iii) _____

   (d) List three illnesses caused by type C micro-organism.
   (i) _____ (ii) _____ (iii) _____

4. Give two examples of fungi.
   (a) _____
   (b) _____

5. How does our skin protect us against micro-organisms? _____
   _____

6. How does our blood protect us against micro-organisms? _____
   _____

7. How do we become immune to some viruses? _____
   _____

8. Why is it important to wash your hands regularly? _____
   _____

9. What is a genetic disease? Give an example. _____
   _____

10. Name two environmental factors that impact on human health.
    (a) _____ (b) _____

11. Plan a healthy menu for an active teenager for an entire day. _____
    _____
    _____
    _____
    _____

12. Give three ways in which we benefit from regular exercise.
    (a) _____
    (b) _____
    (c) _____

13. List three things you can do to boost your mental health.
    (a) _____
    (b) _____
    (c) _____

Knowledge and Understanding

Case Study: The discovery of micro-organisms

Micro-organisms are thought to be the earliest form of life on Earth. However, they were not discovered until relatively recently because they are microscopic. Three scientists contributed to their discovery. In the 1600's Francesco Redi showed that life comes from life. When he stopped flies landing on rotting meat, no maggots appeared. This showed that maggots grow from tiny eggs that flies lay on rotting meat. This didn't explain how smaller micro-organisms like bacteria suddenly appear. People still thought they were spontaneously generated.

In the 1700's Lazzaro Spallanzani showed that micro-organisms are carried in the air. He boiled two flasks with chicken broth. He sealed one from the air and left the other flask open. Micro-organisms only grew on the chicken broth that was open to the air. People still argued that the micro-organisms were growing spontaneously; they thought the micro-organisms didn't grow because they didn't have the air they needed.

In the 1800's Louis Pasteur showed that the micro-organisms were being transported on dust particles in the air. He set up two flasks as shown in Fig. 1 on page 51. Pasteur boiled up the chicken broth. He then left both flasks open to the air through tubes. However, he curved the tube going into the second flask into an S shape. The bend in the tube acted as a trap. The air could travel through freely but the dust particles in the air became trapped. Micro-organisms only grew in the first flask. To further support his theory, Pasteur turned the second flask on its side allowing the chicken broth to touch the trapped dust particles. After a few days micro-organisms did start to grow in the broth in the second flask.

Human Health 15

Questions
1. What did Redi's experiments show?
2. If you were Redi, how would you set up this experiment to ensure that it is a fair test?
3. Why did people accept that micro-organisms are transported in the air when Pasteur published his experiment results but not when Spallanzani published his?
4. What conditions do micro-organisms need to grow?
5. How do you think Spallanzani and Pasteur's experiments have been applied to the food industry?

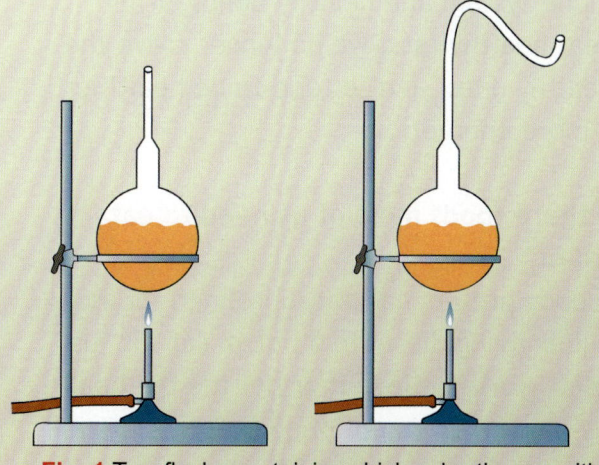

Fig. 1 Two flasks containing chicken broth, one with an S-shaped tube.

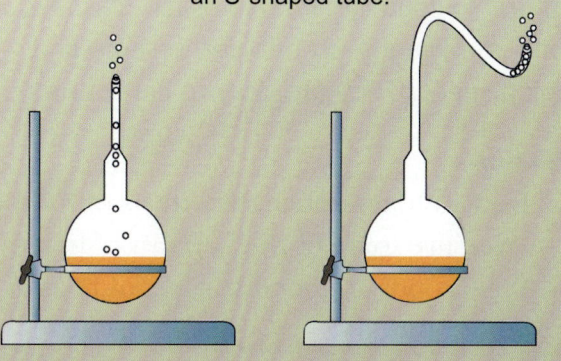

Fig. 2 After a few days micro-organisms only grew in the flask with the straight tube.

Case Study   Healthy fats

This is an extract from an interview with Irene Steffens, a nutritional therapist in Cork.

Do you think the food that teenagers eat affects their health?
Yes, absolutely! Regardless of our age, the food we eat directly affects our health. The effect of what we consume isn't always obvious. Some reactions are immediate, some are very slow. If you have a peanut allergy and you eat peanuts you will become very ill very quickly. Other food allergies or intolerances take a longer time to show symptoms. The foods teenagers eat on a daily basis can either help their bodies to function very well allowing them to have great energy and vibrancy, or they can slowly make their bodies tired, sluggish and ill.

Apart from significantly reducing sugar in the diet, what would you change about the diet of the average teenager?
I would encourage teenagers to eat more avocados, oily fish, nuts and seeds. These foods are high in healthy fats. Healthy fats are so important to the teenage body and brain. Teenagers are trying to concentrate, retain and then reproduce large quantities of information during school and homework hours. This requires brain power. These foods are also packed full of protein, and important minerals like zinc, selenium, calcium and magnesium, which are needed for things like good mental health, a strong

immune system and healthy bones. When we eat healthy fats, we no longer crave the unhealthy ones, and so tend to be healthier and more energetic.

Are there foods most of us need to eat more of?
The body prefers natural, unrefined foods. Imagine giving diesel to a petrol car – it just doesn't work. Believe it or not it's the healthy fatty foods that I mentioned before that we need more of. A variety of fresh, raw nuts and seeds are so good for us, like brazil, cashew, almond and walnuts, sunflower, sesame and pumpkin seeds. They are easy to carry around and snack on when out and about. Throw in some fresh fruit and you're set for the day!

What do you think schools can do to promote good food habits in their students?
Make healthy foods easily accessible, and remove the junk. Consult nutritional therapists and healthy food caterers to get ideas for the canteen. Homemade soups, wholegrain rolls and sandwiches, nuts, seeds, fresh fruit and tasty salads. The possibilities are endless. Remember that the body has to function completely on what we consume, so it would be logical to assume that what we eat affects every function of the body.

Questions
1. Do we always notice the effects of food on our body? Explain.
2. What are some of the benefits of healthy fats?
3. What foods are good sources of healthy fats?

Analyse and Interpret

Answer the following questions related to the cover of a brochure produced by the National Youth Council of Ireland shown here.
1. What message is the cover trying to communicate?
2. Do you think the images on the cover communicate the message well?
3. Why should people make the health changes suggested on the brochure cover?
4. What additional messages do you think should be communicated to young people about their health?

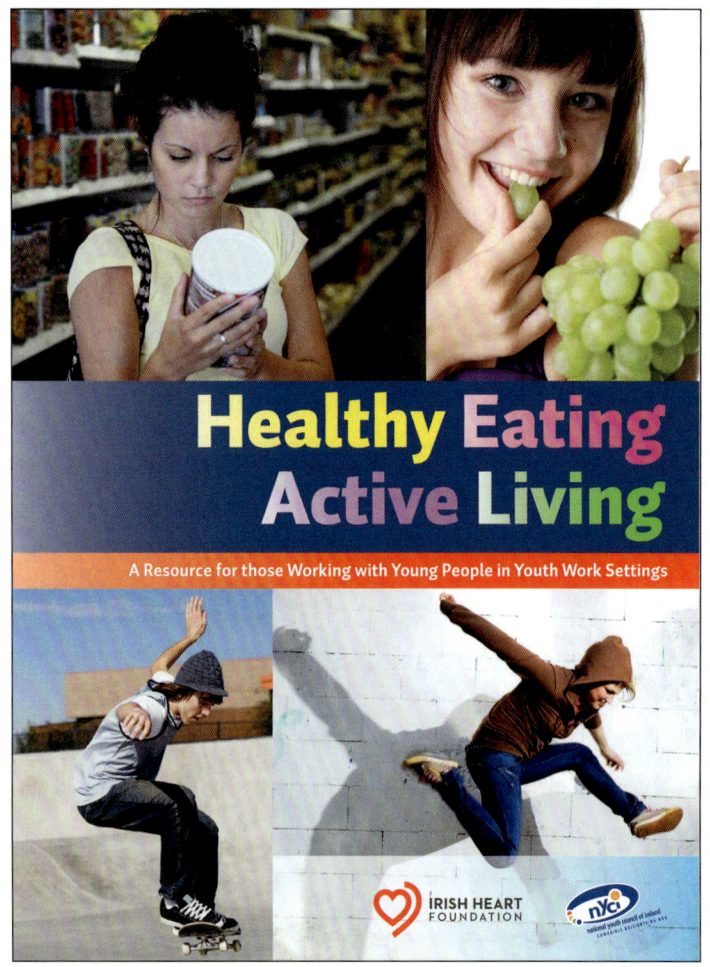

16 Studying Habitats and their Communities

Review Questions

1. Select the correct answer for each of these questions:
   (a) The place where a plant or animal lives:
   - ☐ Ecosystem
   - ☐ Site
   - ☐ Habitat
   - ☐ Community

   (b) A group of organisms and their environment:
   - ☐ Ecosystem
   - ☐ Site
   - ☐ Habitat
   - ☐ Community

   (c) Plants can make their own food. They are called:
   - ☐ Consumers
   - ☐ Producers
   - ☐ Predators
   - ☐ Prey

   (d) An organism that kills and eats another for food:
   - ☐ Consumer
   - ☐ Producer
   - ☐ Predator
   - ☐ Prey

   (e) The thick fur of a polar bear is an _____ to its environment:
   - ☐ Adjustment
   - ☐ Change
   - ☐ Adaptation
   - ☐ Alteration

2. Name (a) two types of habitats and (b) two ecosystems.
   (a) (i) _____ (ii) _____
   (b) (i) _____ (ii) _____

3. Barn owls do not build a nest; instead they use ledges for laying eggs. They feed on small mammals such as mice, rats and shrews that they hunt in open areas. Suggest the habitat and ecosystem of barn owls. _____

4. List three factors that affect the types of plants and animals that are found in an area.
   (a) _____ (b) _____ (c) _____

5. List five pieces of information that are collected as part of a habitat study.
   (a) _____ (b) _____ (c) _____
   (d) _____ (e) _____

6. Name two producers that you would expect to find in an oak woodland.
(a) _____ (b) _____

7. Name (a) two predators found in Irish woodlands and (b) two predators found on the Irish sea shore.
(a) (i) _____ (ii) _____
(b) (i) _____ (ii) _____

8. Name (a) one species that is a predator and (b) one species that is a decomposer.
(a) _____ (b) _____

9. Name an organism that matches each of these descriptions:
(a) Producer _____ (c) Predator _____
(b) Consumer _____ (d) Prey _____

10. Answer these questions in relation to your habitat study:
(a) Name the habitat that you studied. _____
(b) How did you identify plants and animals? _____
_____

(c) Draw a diagram of any piece of equipment that you used and describe how you used it.

(d) What is meant by adaptation? _____
_____

(e) Give an example of adaptation from the habitat that you studied. _____

(f) What is meant by interdependence? _____

(g) Give an example of interdependence from the habitat that you studied. _____

Studying Habitats and their Communities — 16

Knowledge and Understanding

1. Adaptations provide benefits to plants and animals. Fig. 1 is a photograph of a sloth. Identify one adaptation that sloths have.

2. Figs. 2 and 3 are both photographs of the Arctic fox. One of the photographs shows the fur of the Arctic fox in winter, the other photograph shows its fur in summer.
   (a) Identify which is which and suggest a reason for the difference between the two.
   (b) Explain the advantage that the colouring of the Arctic fox gives.
   (c) Do you think this is an example of an adaptation? Justify your answer

Fig. 1

Fig. 2

Fig. 3

3. Describe how each of the relationships (a)–(h) are interdependent:

Fig. 4 Buffalo and oxpecker birds

Fig. 5 Bee and flower

Fig. 6 Whale and barnacles

(a) Birds eating berries
(b) Oxpecker birds travelling on buffalo
(c) Ladybirds living on plants
(d) Rabbits and foxes
(e) Bees drinking nectar
(f) Lions and hyenas
(g) Blackbirds and ivy
(h) Barnacles and humpback whales

4. Foxes are predators of rabbits.
   (a) What effect would an increase in fox numbers have on the rabbit population of an area?
   (b) Suggest what may happen to the foxes living in an area if a disease led to a rapid decrease in rabbit numbers.
5. Plants are producers. Explain what scientists mean by the term producer.
6. Answer the questions which follow on this food chain:

   (a) Identify the primary consumer.
   (b) How many predators are shown in this food chain?
   (c) Which organism would have the lowest numbers? Explain your choice.
   (d) How does the size of the organisms change as food moves through the food chain?

7. What type of relationship best describes each relationship shown in the photographs (a)–(c).

   (a)   (b)   (c)

8. Compare these pairs of relationships:
   (a) Foxes and rabbits
   (b) Lions and hyenas

17 Biodiversity

Review Questions

1. Explain the term biodiversity. _____
2. Humans rely on ecosystems for many natural resources. Name three of these resources:
   (a) _____ (b) _____ (c) _____
3. Name two human activities that threaten biodiversity:
   (a) _____ (b) _____
4. To feed the world's growing population humans need to produce enough _____ and _____ ecological biodiversity for the future.
5. What effect does clearing land for agriculture have on biodiversity?
   _____
6. Identify one way that Coillte tries to improve biodiversity in Ireland.
   _____
7. Identify one practice in modern agriculture that increases crop production but has a negative impact on biodiversity. _____
8. Increased hunting can lead to the _____ of a species.
9. Identify one way that fishermen can help to protect the biodiversity of the oceans.
   _____
10. Name the organisation that is responsible for monitoring the species of plants and animals in Ireland. _____

Knowledge and Understanding

Case Study   Crocodiles and biodiversity in African waterways

The African catfish usually grows to about 30 kg. Due to its large size and efficiency as a predator the catfish has the ability to greatly reduce biodiversity. Catfish feed aggressively on smaller fish and even fish eggs. The only predators capable of killing the largest catfish are Nile

Fig. 1 The Nile crocodile and the African catfish.

crocodiles, humans and perhaps otters. By feeding on the large catfish, crocodiles help to control the negative impact of the catfish on African waterways and therefore help to maintain biodiversity.

Questions
1. Identify two foods that catfish feed on.
2. Name a species that helps to control catfish numbers.
3. What problem could be caused by high numbers of catfish?

Case Study — Pollution: Fish killed in slurry spill

Salmon and trout stocks in a section of the Loobagh river in Kilmallock have almost been wiped out following a slurry spill this week. About 650 adult salmon and trout and countless juveniles were killed. The source of the pollution has been traced to a farm, and an investigation is ongoing.

'It is affecting a couple of miles of river,' explained Mike Fitzsimons, senior fisheries environment officer with Inland Fisheries Ireland.

'We found the source of the pollution so that has been stopped. There is a plume of pollution moving downriver but that has lost a lot of its strength.'

Eamon O'Riordan, chairman of Kilmallock and Kilfinane Anglers Association, came upon the spill at Riversfield bridge in Kilmallock.

He told the *Limerick Post*: 'The sight that greeted me wasn't pleasant. There were a lot of fish dead and lots of fish struggling to get oxygen. The river as a fishing amenity will be wiped out for the next three to four years. It's a sad state of affairs.'

The polluted site lies just 100 metres from the water treatment plant at Kilmallock, which was temporarily shut down.

A spokesperson for Irish Water said: 'The plant was shut down and switched over to a reserve supply at Jamestown. The water supply to Kilmallock was not affected and there was no disruption to the water supply.'

By Kathy Masterson, *Limerick Post* (adapted)

Questions
1. Name two species that were affected by this pollution.
2. What was the source of the pollution?
3. Outline the long-term effects that the pollution could have on the waterway.

Biodiversity 17

Case Study — Education: Protecting the Amazon rainforest

The Amazon Region Protected Areas (ARPA) programme is a conservation programme that is funded by several partners including the Brazilian Government and the World Bank. It has created a number of protected areas where natural resources are sustainably managed. The programme covers almost 70 million hectares of Amazon rainforest in Brazil. Since 2002 local communities have been consulted and involved in designing conservation projects and deciding how the land should be used.

Some areas have been set aside for conservation parks while other areas have been designated for sustainable use by carefully managing activities such as rubber tapping and farming.

Local communities have been trained in agricultural techniques that have a lower impact on the forest. In addition they have learned how to prevent and extinguish forest fires. These strategies have helped to reduce deforestation and improve livelihoods.

Questions

1. Would you agree that this is a 'success story'? Support your answer with information from the case study.
2. Suggest reasons why this conservation approach has been effective.
3. How could satellites be used to help this project?
4. Outline the benefits that this conservation approach could have in the future.
5. Projects that involve communities are being used in conservation all around the world. Find out about one of these projects and explain to the class how it works.

Case Study — Cargo ships in California slow down to protect endangered blue whales

The massive container ships passing through the Santa Barbara Channel off the coast of Southern California will be paid a bonus of $2,500 per trip to slow down, in an effort to cut offshore air pollution and reduce collisions with whales. The four-month pilot programme began in July and is run by federal and local officials as well as an environmental group. It comes as the season for whales in the channel peaks. Last week, a dead fin whale washed up at the beach and harbour city of Port Hueneme, south of Santa Barbara.

'Slowing down ships is a good thing for air pollution, protecting endangered species and human health,' said Kristi Birney, marine conservation analyst with the Environmental Defence Centre based in Santa Barbara.

Six shipping companies have agreed to participate in the programme. The purpose is to reduce exhaust emissions from the ships, which account for half of the ozone pollution in Santa Barbara County, and to protect whales, which are often found washed up on the shore with blunt force trauma from collisions. The timing coincides with the busiest whale-feeding season in the channel, and could save lives among endangered blue whales.

'The estimated population of blue whales in this part of the Pacific is 2,500, so every whale counts toward this population moving off the endangered species list,' said Sean Hastings from the National Oceanic and Atmospheric Administration (NOAA).

About 5,000 ships pass through the Santa Barbara Channel each year to the Los Angeles and Long Beach ports, a 209 km stretch.

Participating ships will be paid $2,500 for slowing to 12 knots during that part of the trip, from more typical speeds of 14 to 18 knots. A similar programme targets air pollution at the Ports of Los Angeles and Long Beach.

The $2,500 bonuses will not be enough to fully cover the lost time to shippers who slow down but it is hoped the incentive will still work. The programme is a way to reward shippers willing to try to avoid colliding with whales.

By Dana Feldman, Reuters

Questions
1. What are the aims of this project?
2. What incentive is being used to motivate ship companies to slow down?
3. What is significant about the timing of this trial?
4. Do you think that paying bonuses to shipping companies to slow down is a suitable approach to the issue of whales being hit by large ships in this area?

18 Mass and Matter

Review Questions

1. What is matter? _____
   _____
2. What is mass? _____
   _____
3. What is the SI unit of mass? _____
4. How many grams are there in a kilogram? _____
5. Name two instruments that can be used to measure mass. (a) _____
   (b) _____
6. What causes an object to have weight? _____
7. What are the three states of matter? (a) _____
   (b) _____
   (c) _____

Knowledge and Understanding

1. Draw diagrams to show the arrangement and movement of particles in a solid, a liquid and a gas.
2. Complete the table below using the following terms: Liquid, Gas, Definite shape, No definite shape, Able to flow, Not able to flow, Easily compressed, Not easily compressed

Solid		
	No definite shape	
		Able to flow
	Not easily compressed	

3. What terms are used to describe the following changes of state?
   (a) Solid → Liquid
   (b) Liquid → Gas
   (c) Liquid → Solid
   (d) Gas → Liquid

4. What terms are used to describe the temperatures at which the following changes of state occur?
   (a) Solid → Liquid
   (b) Liquid → Gas
   (c) Liquid → Solid

5. Explain what happens to the particles in a liquid while it is freezing.

6. Explain what happens to the particles in a gas while it is condensing.

7. The diagrams to the right show the arrangement of particles in a solid, a liquid and a gas. Which of the three diagrams shows a solid? Name the change that takes place when C changes into B.

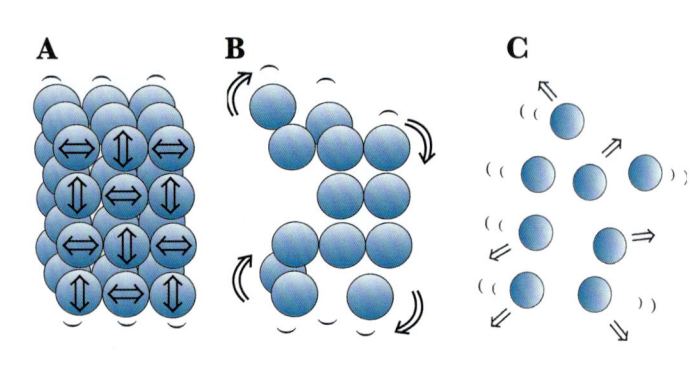

8. The diagrams to the right represent the particles in a gas and in a solid. Explain how these models help to explain the difference between the shapes of gases and solid.

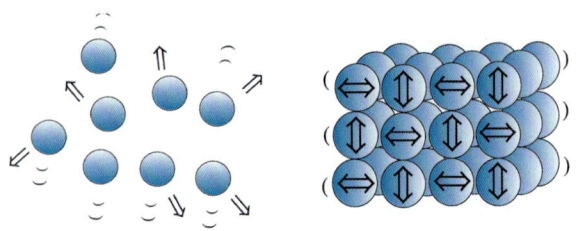

Particles of a gas   **Particles of a solid**

9. The photograph to the right shows a broken glass. Would you expect the mass of glass to be different after the glass breaks? Give a reason for your answer.

10. The photograph to the right shows an ice cream cone melting. Before it began melting, the mass of the ice cream was 100 g.

  (a) When it has completely melted what would you expect the mass of the ice cream to be? Give a reason for your answer.

  (b) A day after the ice cream melted a scientist scraped up all of the remains of the ice cream and found that the mass was 63 g. If the ice cream was untouched explain the reason for the change in mass.

Mass and Matter 18

11. Photograph **A** shows a beaker of water and a dish of salt on an electronic balance. In Photograph **B** the salt has been added to the beaker of water. Describe what happened to the salt and explain how this illustrates the idea of conservation of mass.

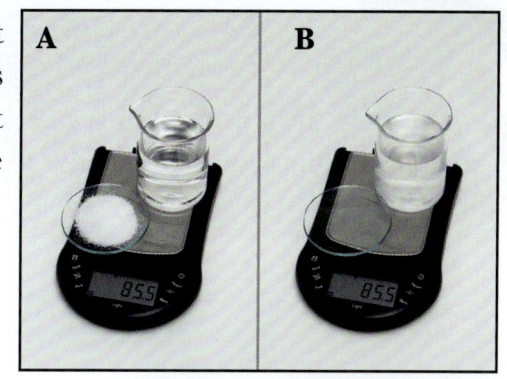

12. The photograph to the right shows a boiling kettle with steam coming out of the spout.
    (**a**) What is steam made of?
    (**b**) Look carefully at the end of the spout of the kettle. Explain why there is no steam at this exact spot.
    (**c**) Describe two changes of state that are taking place while this kettle is boiling.

13. An instant cold pack is a device that consists of two bags. One bag contains water and lies inside another bag containing ammonium nitrate. When the inner bag of water is broken by squeezing the package, the water reacts with the ammonium nitrate causing the contents to become cold.
    Would you expect the mass of the cold pack to change while being used? Give a reason for your answer.

19 Classifying Materials

Review Questions

1. What do scientists mean by a pure substance? _____
   _____

2. What is the difference between a mixture and a compound? _____
   _____
   _____

3. What is an element? _____
   _____

4. Distinguish between a physical change and a chemical change. _____
   _____
   _____

5. Classify the following as either a physical change (P) or a chemical change (C).

   (a) Milk spoils/goes off in the fridge _____
   (b) Chocolate goes soft in the hot sun _____
   (c) Two <u>colourless</u> liquids are mixed together and turn <u>purple</u> _____
   (d) Leaves change from green to red _____
   (e) Metal on a car turns from silver to reddish-brown _____
   (f) Water disappears from a glass over time _____
   (g) Sawdust forms from wood being cut with a saw _____
   (h) Ice breaks into smaller pieces _____
   (i) Carbon dioxide is dissolved to make fizzy drinks _____
   (j) Water boils _____
   (k) Clothes are torn _____
   (l) A match is lit _____
   (m) Food is chewed _____
   (n) Ice cream melts _____
   (o) A rubber band is stretched _____

6. What elements are represented by the following symbols?
   (a) Cu _____   (c) Zn _____   (e) Al _____
   (b) Fe _____   (d) Ag _____   (f) Au _____

Classifying Materials 19

Knowledge and Understanding

1. The photograph below shows a single candle at three different stages of burning.

   (a) Describe the physical changes that take place during this process.
   (b) Describe the chemical changes that take place during this process.
   (c) Would you expect the total mass of the wax shown in the second candle to be the same as the total mass of wax in the third candle? Give a reason for your answer.

2. The photograph below shows two nails before and after rusting. Rusting is a chemical change. The iron in the nails reacts with oxygen in the air to form a new compound called iron oxide. Would you expect the mass of the nails to be the same after rusting? Give a reason for your answer.

Case Study: The discovery of titanium

Titanium is the ninth most abundant element on Earth. In 1791, an amateur geologist, Reverend William Gregor, from Cornwall in England found a magnetic sand that looked like gunpowder. He analysed the sand and found that it was a mixture of a compound called magnetite (the old name for a compound made from iron and oxygen) and another compound. This other compound was reddish-brown in colour and he concluded that it was made from a new unknown metal element and oxygen. Gregor called this new element manaccanite in honour of his Parish (Manaccan) in Cornwall.

Four years later, a German chemist called Martin Klaproth analysed a mineral with the same reddish-brown compound and also found a new element. He called his new element titanium. When Klaproth received a copy of the paper that Gregor had written in 1791 he realised that they had both discovered the same element and that Gregor had been first. However scientists preferred Klaproth's choice of name so element 22 on the Periodic Table is called titanium.

It took another 119 years before a 99.9% pure sample of the element titanium was extracted. Matthew Hunter heated up a compound of titanium chloride with the element sodium under pressure. A chemical reaction took place and the product was an almost pure sample of titanium. By 1936 scientists had worked out a new method to extract large amounts of titanium from its compounds.

Titanium is very light but extremely strong. It does not corrode easily. Even the salty sea which rusts iron very quickly doesn't affect it. In fact, if you leave titanium under the sea for 4,000 years, only a layer on the surface the thickness of this page will corrode. It can be mixed with iron and aluminium to make strong but light structures such as jet engines and spacecraft. It is also used to build artificial limbs, hip and knee replacements and the frames of some bicycles. When it is in a compound with oxygen called titania (titanium dioxide), it is used in white paint, in sunscreen and in toothpaste (it is considered to be non-toxic).

Questions

1. Name two compounds and three elements mentioned in the article.
2. Was the initial substance that Gregor found an element, a compound or a mixture?
3. How do we know a chemical reaction took place when Hunter heated up the titanium chloride?
4. How does the atomic nature of matter explain why titanium metal has different uses from the compound titania?
5. Write a short article that you think Gregor might have written in 1791 for a scientific journal when he discovered titanium.
6. How does the story above show that advances in scientific knowledge take place over time?

20 Mixtures

Review Questions

1. What is a mixture? _____
   _____

2. What is a solution? _____
   _____

3. Give three examples of mixtures or solutions.
   (a) _____
   (b) _____
   (c) _____

4. In a saline solution (salt and water) what is the (a) solute and (b) solvent?
   (a) _____
   (b) _____

Knowledge and Understanding

1. Describe, with the aid of a diagram, how a mixture of sand and water could be separated.
2. Give two ways in which a soluble solid can be separated from a liquid.
3. Which of the two methods given in Question 2 would you use if you wanted to keep the liquid?
4. Draw the apparatus you would use to carry out a distillation. Label each part and describe its function.
5. What is observed when black ink is used in a chromatography experiment? Explain this observation.

Analyse and Interpret

1. Taylor heard a cry of dismay from the kitchen and came running. 'What happened?' she asked her mum. 'Your little sister has been playing in the kitchen and has mixed up all the salt and pepper,' her mum replied. 'How will we separate them again?'
   Taylor conducted a couple of quick experiments and discovered that while salt dissolves in water, pepper floats to the top. Taylor told her mum, 'Don't worry, I think I have a solution.'
   (a) How do you think Taylor discovered that salt dissolves in water and pepper does not?
   (b) Having discovered this difference between the salt and the pepper, how do you think Taylor can separate them?

2. In order for the water supplied to our homes to be safe to drink it has to be treated. It is first screened through wire mesh to remove large pieces of dirt and rubbish. The water is then allowed to settle in reservoirs for a time to enable insoluble substances to settle to the bottom. The water is then pumped to filtration beds. These contain sand and gravel. The sand is very fine and works a little like filter paper. Finally some chlorine is added to kill bacteria and fluoride is added to prevent dental decay.

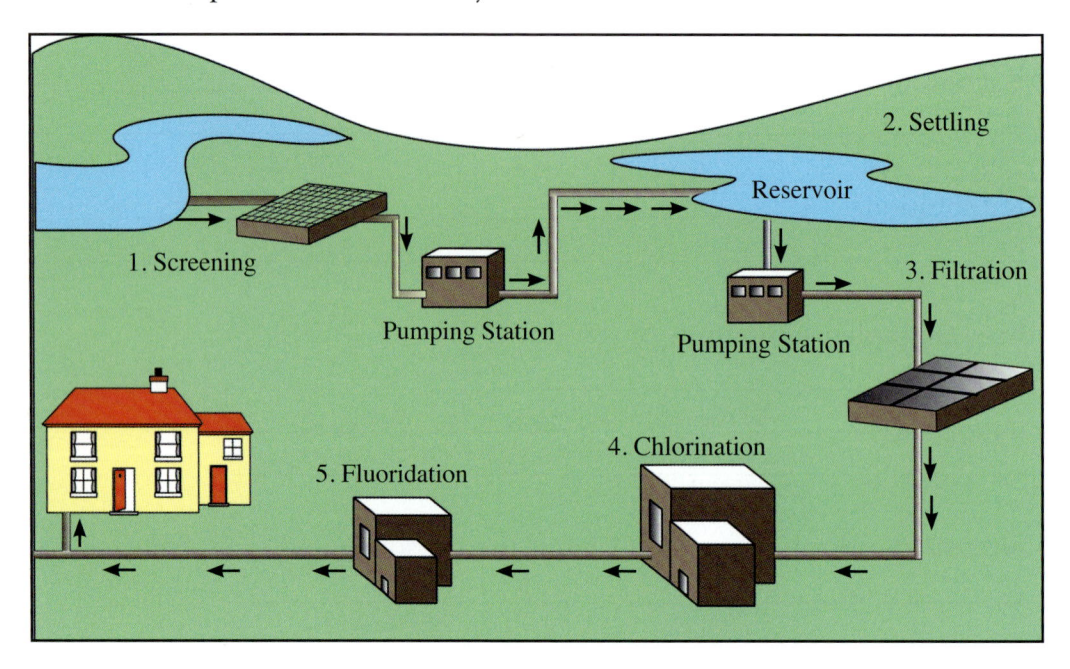

(**a**) Why do you think the water is screened before it is filtered?
(**b**) Why is it important to allow the water to settle for some time?
(**c**) If you were designing a water treatment plant would you take water from the top, middle or bottom of the reservoir for filtration? Why?
(**d**) What types of materials are removed by filtration?
(**e**) How would the sand and gravel work like filter paper?
(**f**) It is necessary to wash the sand and gravel from time to time. Why do you think this is?
(**g**) Before the water is sent to people's homes it has to be treated with chlorine. Why?
(**h**) What is the purpose of adding fluoride to the water?

3. Carol is participating in a round-the-world yacht race. She has this piece of equipment with her in case she gets lost at sea. (a) What do you think it is for? (b) How does it work?

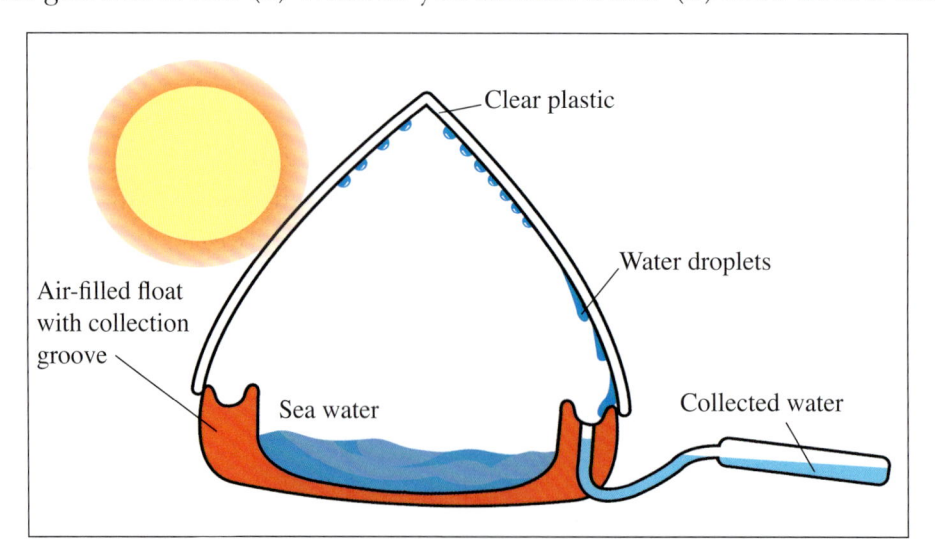

Mixtures 20

4. Graffiti made in black marker has been found in the science laboratory. The teacher knows which class it happened in. All the students are asked to open their pencil cases and hand the teacher their black markers.
   (a) Which students have markers that have yellow in the black ink?
   (b) What colours make up the ink in Jordan's marker?
   (c) Name two students who use the same brand of marker.
   (d) The result of the teacher's enquiry is shown below. Who do you think was responsible?

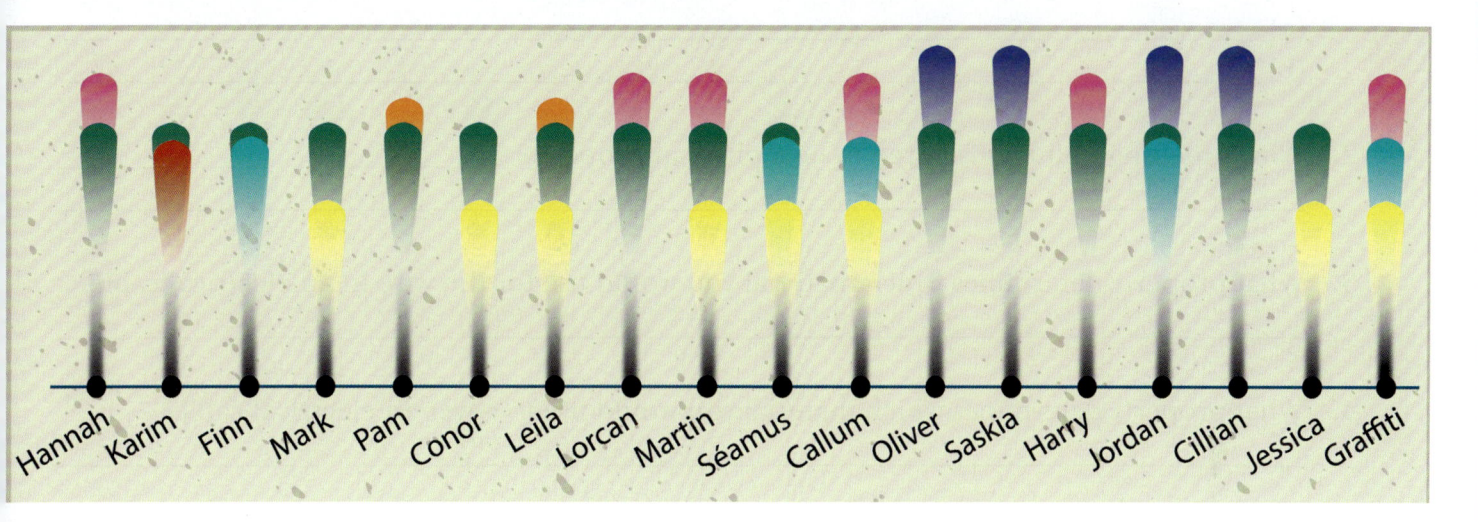

21 Properties of Materials

Review Questions

1. Explain the terms (a) physical property (b) chemical property.
   (a) _____
   (b) _____

2. Why is melting point considered to be a physical property? _____
   _____

3. What property determines which material you would use for the wire in an electrical cable?
   _____

4. What property determines which material you would use to cover an electrical cable?
   _____

5. Which of the following properties of hydrogen is a chemical property?
   (a) It is a gas. ☐
   (b) It is colourless. ☐
   (c) It can burn and even explode in the presence of air. ☐

6. What property must a substance have if you want to make a solution of it in water?
   _____

Knowledge and Understanding

1. Explain how a scientist might set up an experiment to tell two different white powders apart on the basis of their melting points.
2. Describe how crystals form.
3. Why would a saucepan be designed with an iron base and a wooden handle?

Case Study — Insulating your home

It is estimated that about 60 per cent of the total energy usage in a home goes on heating. It makes sense then to reduce the need for heating by improving the insulation. It is likely that most houses now have some form of attic insulation, given that it is one of the easiest ways to prevent heat escaping from a house. But is it enough?

Typically, it was recommended that attics are

Properties of Materials 21

insulated with 150 mm of product such as sheep's wool or polystyrene. Now, however, experts recommend you bring it up to 300 mm. Some other materials have less thermal conductivity and as a result you don't need the same thickness to achieve the same result.

The Sustainable Energy Authority of Ireland (SEAI) estimates a 54 m² attic will cost you about €400 to insulate, but could save about €130 a year in heating costs.

From *The Irish Times* (adapted)

Questions
(a) What property determines whether a material is a good insulator or not?
(b) What percentage of our home energy usage goes to heating our homes?
(c) What is the easiest way for heat to escape from our homes?
(d) Identify two factors that improve the insulating ability of a material.
(e) Use the information from SEAI in the article to calculate how many years it would take to recover the cost of insulating a 54 m² attic through the savings made on heating bills.

Analyse and Interpret

1. The table below gives information about the solubilities of a range of chemicals in water at 20°C. Answer the questions below.

Chemical	Solubility (g/100 cm³)
Copper sulfate	32
Glucose	90
Sucrose	202

Chemical	Solubility (g/100 cm³)
Copper chloride	73
Aluminium chloride	46
Iron sulfate	40

(a) Organise the chemicals in order of least soluble to most soluble.
(b) Describe how a scientist could carry out an experiment to find out the solubility of the chemicals at 20°C.
(c) What would be seen in a beaker containing 60 g of iron sulfate in 100 cm³ of water at 20°C?
(d) Present the information contained in the table as a bar chart.
(e) How much copper sulfate could a scientist add to 50 cm³ of water before a saturated solution formed at 20°C?

2. The table below shows how the solubility of potassium iodide in water changes with temperature.

Temperature (°C)	Solubility (g/100 cm^3)
10	136
20	144
30	153
40	162
50	169
60	176
70	184
80	192
90	198
100	202

(a) Draw a trend graph of the data in the table above.
(b) Describe the relationship between temperature and solubility.
(c) How does your graph support your answer to part (b)?

22 Structure of the Atom

Review Questions

1. What are the three types of sub-atomic particle in an atom?
   (a) _____
   (b) _____
   (c) _____

2. Compare the three particles in Question 1 on the basis of mass, location and charge by filling in the table: (a) _____ (b) _____ (c) _____

Mass			
Location			
Charge			

3. Which sub-atomic particle has the smallest mass? _____
4. If you know the atomic number and the mass number of an atom how can you work out the number of neutrons in the nucleus of that atom? _____
5. How many energy levels are needed to hold the first 13 electrons? _____
6. Which element normally has 13 electrons in each of its atoms? _____
7. Complete the table by filling in the number of protons, electrons and neutrons for an atom of each element:

	Phosphorus	Silicon	Argon	Beryllium
Protons				
Electrons				
Neutrons				

8. Draw a diagram of an atom of sulfur.

9. Identify the following atoms.

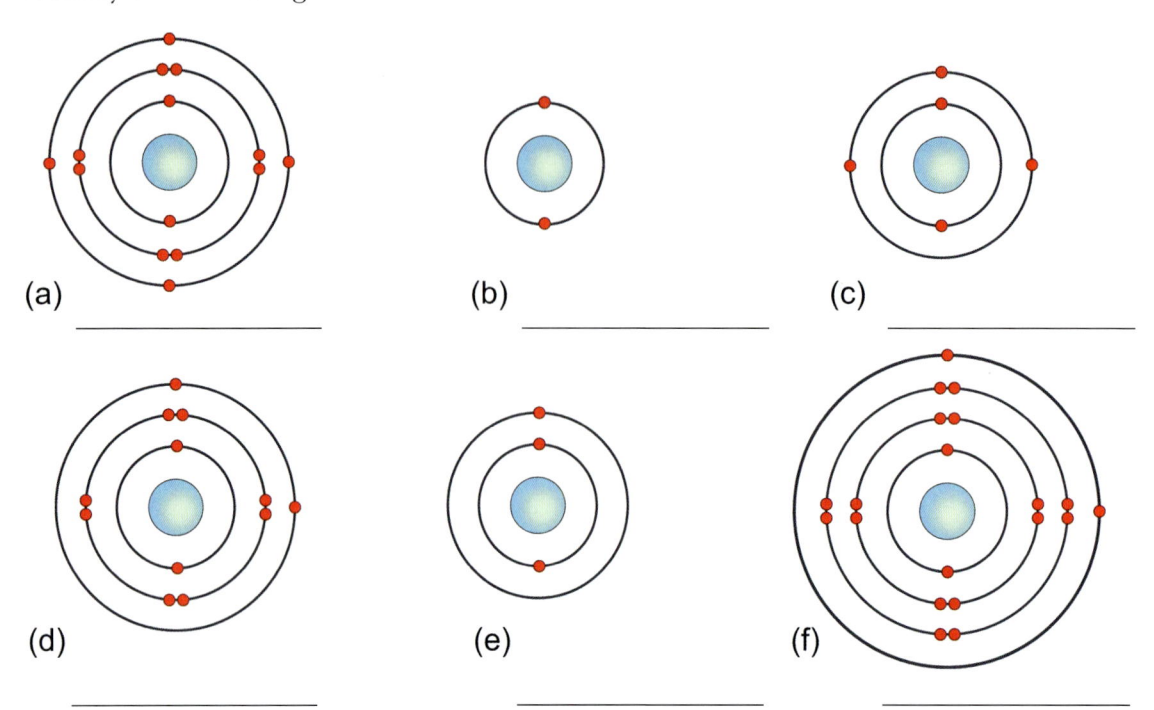

(a) _____   (b) _____   (c) _____

(d) _____   (e) _____   (f) _____

Knowledge and Understanding

Case Study: The history of the atom

The idea of the atom has been fascinating scientists for hundreds of years. The name atom comes from a Greek word *atomos* which means 'cannot be split'. Ancient Greek philosophers thought that matter was made up of atoms which were tiny and couldn't be broken down into simpler or smaller things.

Many centuries later scientists tried to find out what atoms were made of. The first sub-atomic particle that was discovered was the electron. In 1897 Joseph Thomson found out that electrons are very tiny, negatively charged particles. He knew atoms had no overall charge so he suggested that an atom looked like the diagram in Fig. 1.

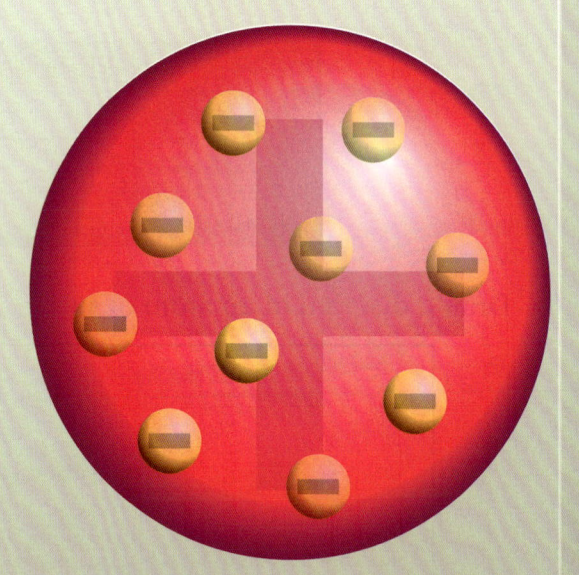

Fig. 1 Joseph Thomson's plum pudding model of the atom.

Structure of the Atom 22

This model was called the plum pudding model because Thomson described the atom as being a sphere of positive charge with electrons stuck in it like currants.

A scientist called Ernest Rutherford then carried out more experiments and found that atoms are mostly empty space. He suggested that almost all the mass of an atom is in a nucleus. He drew a model of the atom which looked like the diagram in Fig. 2

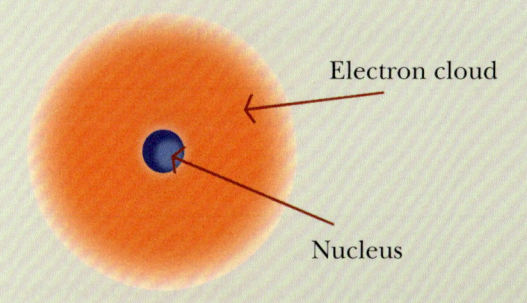

Fig. 2 Rutherford's model of the atom.

Rutherford carried out more experiments and discovered that the nucleus of an atom has particles that have a positive charge and other particles that have no charge.

In 1912 Niels Bohr suggested a model of the atom which had some particles in the nucleus with electrons arranged in energy levels around the outside.

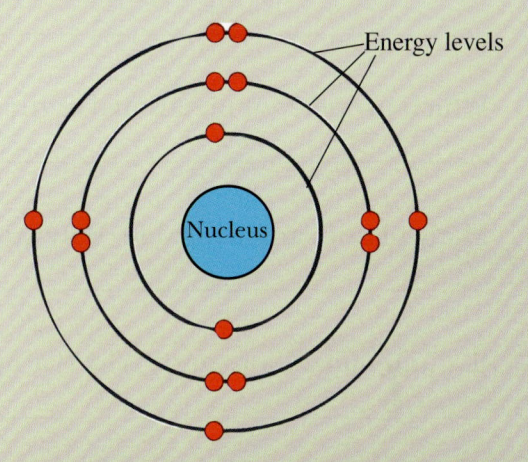

Fig. 3 A Bohr diagram of an atom of phosphorus.

Since then scientists have continued to develop models of the atom that are more and more complex. However, Bohr's model is still used today as it helps to explain how atoms join together with other atoms in a clear and simple way.

Questions
1. How did the Greek philosophers describe atoms? Were they correct?
2. Why do we not use the plum pudding model of an atom today?
3. Who discovered the electron?
4. How were electrons first described?
5. (a) Who discovered that atoms have a nucleus?
   (b) What particles did he suggest were held in the nucleus?
6. Name the positively charged particle that is found in the nucleus.
7. Name the particle that is found in the nucleus that has no charge.
8. Who discovered that atoms are mostly empty space?
9. What contribution did Niels Bohr make to the model of the atom?
10. Why do we still use Bohr's model today even though our scientific understanding has developed over time?

23 The Periodic Table and Chemical Formulae

Review Questions

1. Which property of metals makes them suitable for use in electrical wiring?
   _____

2. Which property of metals makes them suitable for use as bells?
   _____

3. Many plastics are malleable. Why are plastics not considered to be metals?
   _____

4. Sodium metal looks grey. Why is it not shiny?
   _____

5. An element is a solid at room temperature. Is it more likely to be a metal or a non-metal?
   _____

6. Many bicycles have steel frames. Iron and steel can corrode. Give a visible sign of corrosion.
   _____

7. Who first proposed the layout of the Periodic Table we use today?
   _____

8. The columns on a Periodic Table are called groups. On what basis are elements put into groups?
   _____

9. Which group or groups of elements tend to lose electrons when combining to form compounds?
   _____

10. Which group or groups tend to gain or share electrons when combining to form compounds?
    _____

11. Which group or groups tend to form compounds only by sharing electrons?
    _____

The Periodic Table and Chemical Formulae 23

Knowledge and Understanding

1. Describe an experiment which helps to show whether or not a material is a metal.
2. Name three of the groups on the Periodic Table and describe their properties.

Analyse and Interpret

1. Using the information given below, write the formula for each ionic compound in the space provided in the table underneath. The first line has been done for you.

Aluminium	Al (loses 3 electrons)	Bromine	Br (gains 1 electron)
Barium	Ba (loses 2 electrons)	Chlorine	Cl (gains 1 electron)
Calcium	Ca (loses 2 electrons)	Iodine	I (gains 1 electron)
Magnesium	Mg (loses 2 electrons)	Fluorine	F (gains 1 electron)
Potassium	K (loses 1 electron)	Nitrogen	N (gains 3 electrons)
Sodium	Na (loses 1 electron)	Oxygen	O (gains 2 electrons)
Lithium	Li (loses 1 electron)	Phosphorus	P (gains 3 electrons)
Iron (II)	Fe (loses 2 electrons)	Sulfur	S (gains 2 electrons)

	Bromine	Chlorine	Iodine	Fluorine	Nitrogen	Oxygen	Phosphorus	Sulfur
Aluminium	$AlBr_3$	$AlCl_3$	AlI_3	AlF_3	AlN	Al_2O_3	AlP	Al_2S_3
Barium								
Calcium								
Magnesium								
Potassium								
Sodium								
Lithium								
Iron (II)								

2. A student set up the following experiment to investigate the rusting of iron nails. A nail was placed in each of three test tubes A, B, and C. Test tube A contained water. Test tube B contained calcium chloride (a compound which dries or removes water vapour from the air). Test tube C contained boiled water with a layer of oil on top. Water that has been boiled for a long time contains very little or no air/oxygen. The oil prevents more air/oxygen from dissolving in the water. After five days the student observed that only the nail in test tube A had formed some rust.

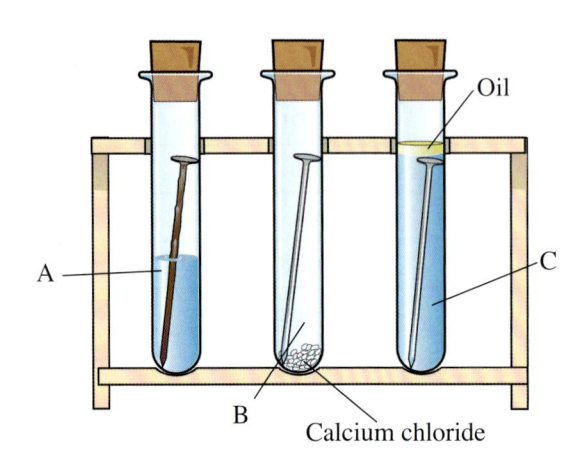

(a) Based on the results of this experiment what conditions appear to be necessary for rusting to occur?
(b) What steps should the student have taken to ensure that this experiment was a fair test?
(c) What could the student have done to make the results more reliable?
(d) Suggest three ways to prevent or slow down the rate at which rust forms.

24 Acids and Bases

Review Questions

1. Select the correct answers for each of these questions:
   (a) The symbol on the right means:
   Toxic ❑   Flammable ❑   Corrosive ❑   None of these ❑
   (b) What taste do acids have?
   Sweet ❑   Sour ❑   Salty ❑   No taste ❑
   (c) Which of these are acids?
   Lemon juice ❑   Vinegar ❑   Oven cleaner ❑   Fizzy drinks ❑
   (d) What word is used to describe a chemical that changes colour in acids and bases?
   Marker ❑   Meter ❑   Indicator ❑   Scale ❑
   (e) What two substances are produced when an acid neutralises a base?
   Salt and oxygen ❑   Salt and water ❑
   Water and carbonate ❑   Soap and carbon dioxide ❑

2. Name an indicator that turns blue in a base. _____

3. To what colour does this indicator change in an acid? _____

Knowledge and Understanding

1. Explain the term indicator.
2. What is the pH scale used to measure?
3. Explain how universal indicator can be used to find the pH of a substance.
4. Why might a scientist use a universal indicator instead of a litmus indicator to test an unknown solution?
5. (a) Name a substance that could be represented by each letter in the diagram below.
   (b) Which letter would represent a stronger acid – A or B?
   (c) Which letter would represent a weaker basic substance – D or E?

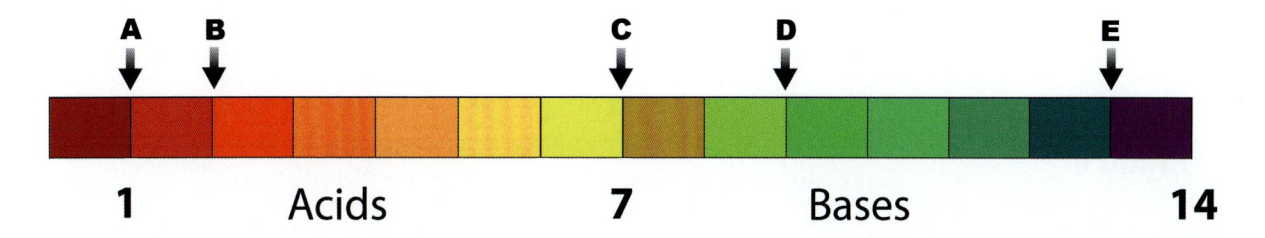

6. What happens in a neutralisation reaction?
7. Indigestion remedies are used to _____ stomach acid. Give one other example of this type of reaction.

8. The diagram below shows the equipment used to carry out a neutralisation reaction between an acid and a base using a titration.

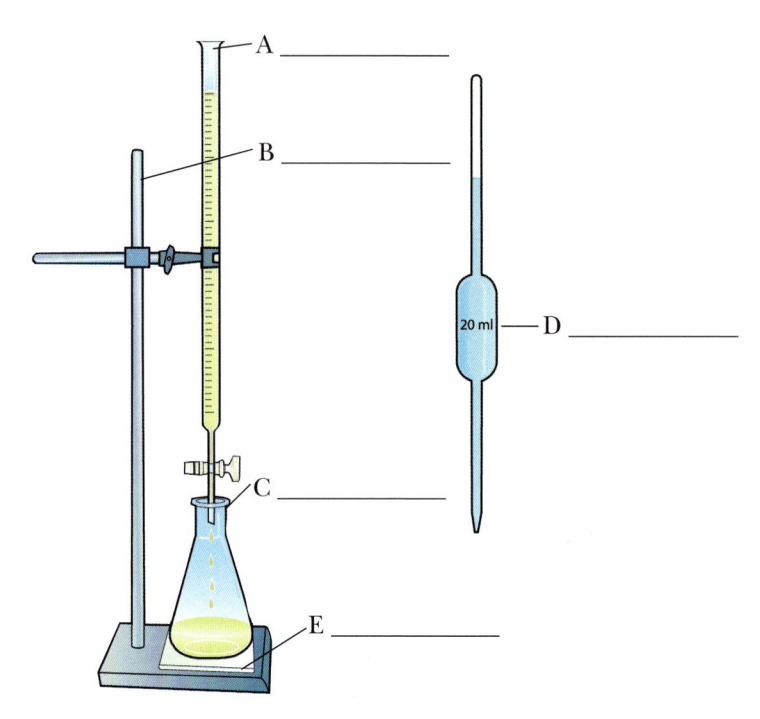

A _____
B _____
D _____
C _____
E _____

(a) Name the parts labelled A – E.
(b) Which piece of equipment measures the volume of acid?
(c) Which piece of equipment measures the volume of base?
(d) Which piece of equipment holds the base?
(e) Where is the indicator added?
(f) What is the purpose of part E?

9. A student designed an experiment to test the effectiveness of different indigestion remedies. The same solution of hydrochloric acid, one tablet of the remedy being tested and 3 drops of methyl orange indicator were used for each test. The endpoint was when the colour changed from yellow to pink. The results are shown in the table:

Indigestion remedy	Volume of acid neutralised (cm^3)	Average volume of acid neutralised (cm^3)
Brand A	12	12.3
	10	
	15	
Brand B	16	13.7
	10	
	15	
Brand C	12	12.3
	13	
	12	
Brand D	10	11.3
	11	
	13	

(a) Based on the information given, do you think the experiment was a fair one? Explain your answer.

(b) The student used a burette with markings at every 1 cm³. Would you describe this instrument as precise?

(c) Both brand A and brand C gave the same average result. Which set of results could be described as more precise – brand A or brand C? Explain your choice.

(d) According to these results the tablets of which brand are (i) the most effective indigestion remedy and (ii) the least effective remedy? Justify your answer.

10. You are given a solution of dilute hydrochloric acid and a range of bases that are all white solids. How could you find out the following:

(a) Which base is the strongest?

(b) What volume of acid is needed to neutralise a solution of each base?

Case Study   Adding lime to soil

Lime is a vital nutrient and is spread over land where soil pH is low. Where the soil pH drops in either grassland or fields that grow grains, the plants cannot take in nutrients from fertilisers as easily.

Phosphorus is the most expensive nutrient and low soil pH reduces the amount that plants absorb. In grassland low pH causes poor recycling of soil mineral nitrogen (N) which is needed by plants for growth. Some crops do not survive if soil pH is low. Barley and wheat are the most sensitive crops to low soil pH.

Liming is the addition of limestone, which contains calcium compounds, to soil. The lime neutralises the soil and raises the pH. Liming soils has many indirect beneficial effects. For example, liming an acid soil increases the population of bacteria, fungi and earthworms, which are responsible for the breakdown of soil organic matter. This process helps to improve both the structure of the soil and the conditions for plant root growth and absorption of nutrients. It is widely recognised that liming heavy soils improves soil structure and makes it easier to prepare soil for planting.

By Mark Plunkett, *Irish Independent* (Adapted)

Questions

1. Will acidic soil have a high or low pH?
2. Is lime added to soils with a low pH or a high pH?
3. From the article find a negative effect of low soil pH.
4. Which cereal crops are identified as being the most affected by low pH?
5. Apart from increasing soil pH, list the other benefits of applying lime to soil.
6. Liming soil is an example of what type of reaction.

25 Chemical Reactions

Review Questions

1. Name four factors that affect the rate of chemical reactions.
   (a) _____ (b) _____ (c) _____
   (d) _____
2. How can carbon dioxide be produced in a laboratory? _____
   _____
   _____
3. What does the term 'biochemical reaction' mean? _____
4. What is an enzyme? _____
5. Give two examples of enzymes.
   (a) _____ (b) _____
6. List two factors that affect the rate of enzyme-controlled reactions.
   (a) _____ (b) _____
7. Distinguish between an exothermic reaction and an endothermic reaction. _____
   _____

Knowledge and Understanding

1. Explain how and why temperature affects the rate of reaction.
2. Explain how and why increasing the concentration of a reactant affects the rate of reaction.
3. What is activation energy?
4. What is an energy profile diagram?

Case Study Dust explosion

On the evening of May 2, 1878 in Minneapolis, a flour mill exploded in a fireball, hurling debris hundreds of feet into the air. In a matter of seconds, a series of thunderous explosions – heard 10 miles away – destroyed the building and several neighbouring ones. It was the worst disaster of its type in the city's history. At six o'clock that evening, the mill's large day crew completed its shift. Fourteen men who made up the night crew arrived. An hour later, three deafening explosions echoed out.

All fourteen workers were killed. Within minutes, the fire had spread to the other mills beside it. They also exploded, killing four more workers.

Chemical Reactions 25

At the inquest into the deaths of the workers, the mill's manager explained that rapidly burning flour dust had caused the disaster. His explanation was later confirmed by two University of Minnesota professors. They carried out a number of experiments that showed that flour could explode easily when separated into tiny particles in the air. This is because they react (burn) much faster when the particle size is smaller. The professors concluded that two of the millstones, running dry, had rubbed against each other, causing a spark that ignited the dust.

The mill owner reopened a new mill in 1880. It was safer and more technologically advanced than the original mill and operated without incident for several more decades.

Adapted from www.mnopedia.org/event/1878-washburn-mill-explosion

Questions
1. Why did the flour dust burn when a bag of flour doesn't?
2. What experiment do you think the two professors from the University of Minnesota might have carried out to prove their theory?
3. Why was it important to carry out experiments to prove their theory?
4. What caused the spark that lit the dust?
5. Why did the dust not burn without the spark?
6. What safety precautions do you think are in place in modern-day mills to prevent explosions such as this from taking place?

Analyse and Interpret

1. When hydrochloric acid (solution) reacts with calcium carbonate (solid), carbon dioxide (gas) is released. The graph below shows the volume of carbon dioxide released (y-axis) against time (x-axis). In each of the cases labelled A, B, C and D the following variables were kept constant: temperature, pressure, volume of hydrochloric acid used, concentration of hydrochloric acid used.

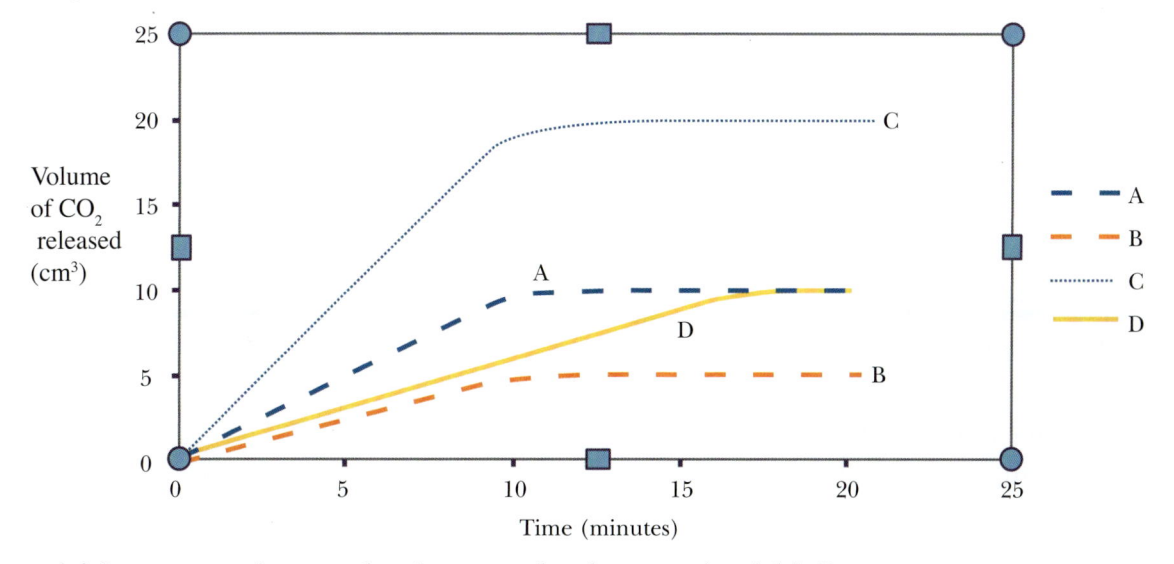

(a) In an experiment what is meant by the term 'variable'?
(b) Why is it important to keep some of the variables constant during an experiment?
(c) List two variables that could have changed in these experiments.

(d) In which case, A, B, C or D, was the least mass of calcium carbonate used? Explain your answer.
(e) Suggest any one difference between the conditions used during case A and the conditions used during case D.
(f) At the start of the reactions, which case, A, B, C or D, showed the greatest rate of reaction?

2. When hydrochloric acid reacts with sodium thiosulfate solution the solution turns from a see-through colourless solution to a cloudy yellow mixture that cannot be seen through. A cross is drawn on a piece of paper and put under the reaction flask. It becomes difficult to see the cross as the reaction progresses.

The experiment was carried out at different temperatures and the following results were obtained:

Temperature (°C)	10	20	30	40	50	60
Time taken for cross to disappear (s)	183	107	63	43	31	25

(a) Draw a graph of the results.
(b) Use the graph to reach a conclusion about how temperature affects the rate of reaction.
(c) When do you think the student started the timer when carrying out the experiment?
(d) When should the student stop the timer?
(e) Do you think this method gives accurate results? How could the accuracy be improved?
(f) List three variables that the student would need to keep constant during this experiment.

3. Match the energy profile diagrams A – C with the reactions (i)–(iii).

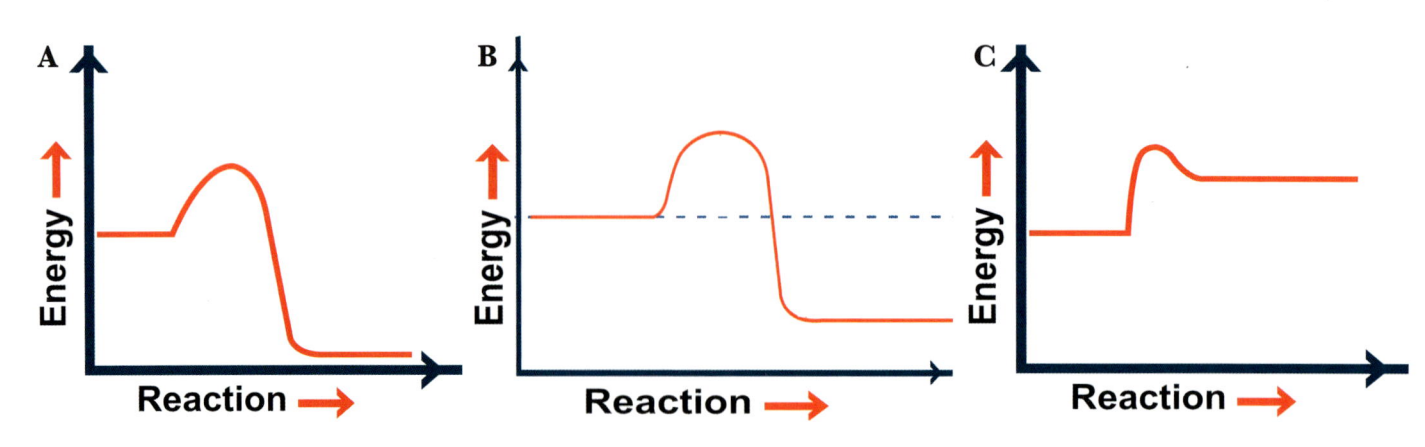

(i) An ice pack is activated.
(ii) A strip of magnesium ribbon is burned giving out a bright white light.
(iii) Dilute hydrochloric acid and dilute sodium hydroxide react together producing a warming effect.

A	
B	
C	

26 Life Cycle of Materials

Review Questions

1. Name two materials commonly used by people.
   (a) _____
   (b) _____

2. (a) What method is used to obtain metals? _____
   (b) Give two negative effects of this method.
      (i) _____
      (ii) _____

3. What raw material is used to make plastics? _____

4. In your opinion what is the worst impact of plastics on the environment? _____
   _____

5. Which of these objects breaks down biologically most quickly – glass bottles, plastic bottles, plastic bags or cotton? _____

6. Name four materials that can be recycled and four materials or objects that cannot be recycled in Ireland.

Recycled in Ireland	Not recycled in Ireland
(a) _____	(a) _____
(b) _____	(b) _____
(c) _____	(c) _____
(d) _____	(d) _____

7. If a material cannot be recycled using the recycling bin where else could it be recycled?
   _____

8. Think of the products that are available in supermarkets.
   (a) Name three products that do not use packaging.
   (b) Name three products that use metal packaging.
   (c) Name three products that use plastic packaging.

No Packaging	Metal Packaging	Plastic Packaging
(i) _____	(i) _____	(i) _____
(ii) _____	(ii) _____	(ii) _____
(iii) _____	(iii) _____	(iii) _____

Knowledge and Understanding

1. A packaging-free supermarket called Original Unverpackt opened in Berlin in 2014. List as many positives and negatives as you can for shopping in this way.
2. A 15 cent plastic bag levy was introduced in Ireland in 2002. This charge has since been increased to 22 cent. How do you think this has affected consumer habits?
3. Waste has the potential to cause a lot of harm to the environment. (a) List five items that you have seen disposed of incorrectly in Ireland. (b) Why is waste sometimes disposed of incorrectly?
4. The diagram in Fig. 1 shows the main stages in the life cycle of all materials.
    (**a**) Give an example of what happens at each stage for one of the following materials:
        wood, aluminium, copper, plastic.
    (**b**) In addition to giving one example of what happens at each stage, identify where energy is used in the life cycle of your chosen product.

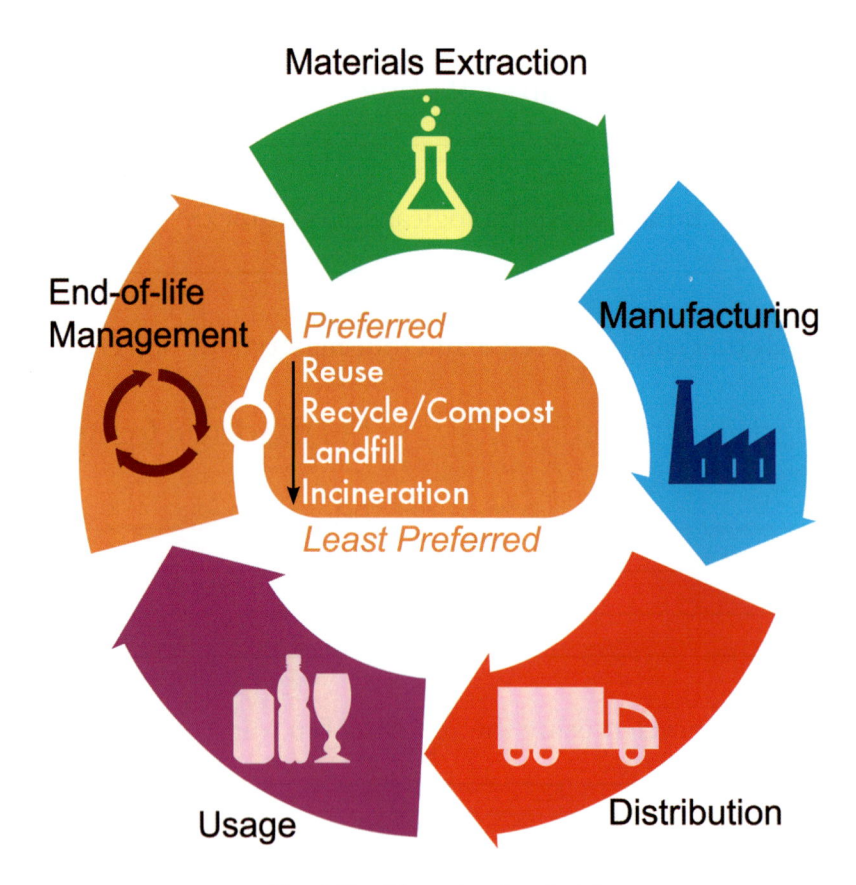

Fig. 1 The life cycle of materials

Life Cycle of Materials 26

Case Study: Waste and recycling in Ireland

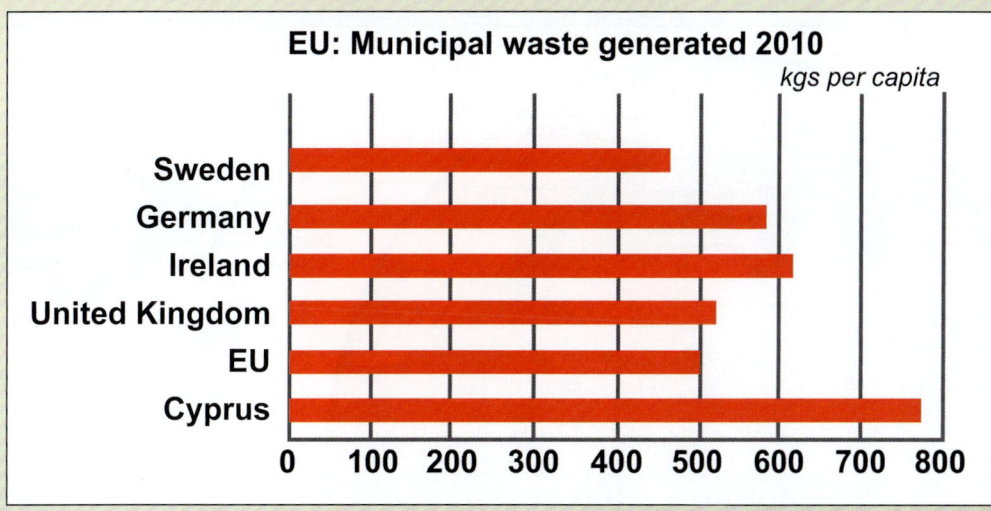

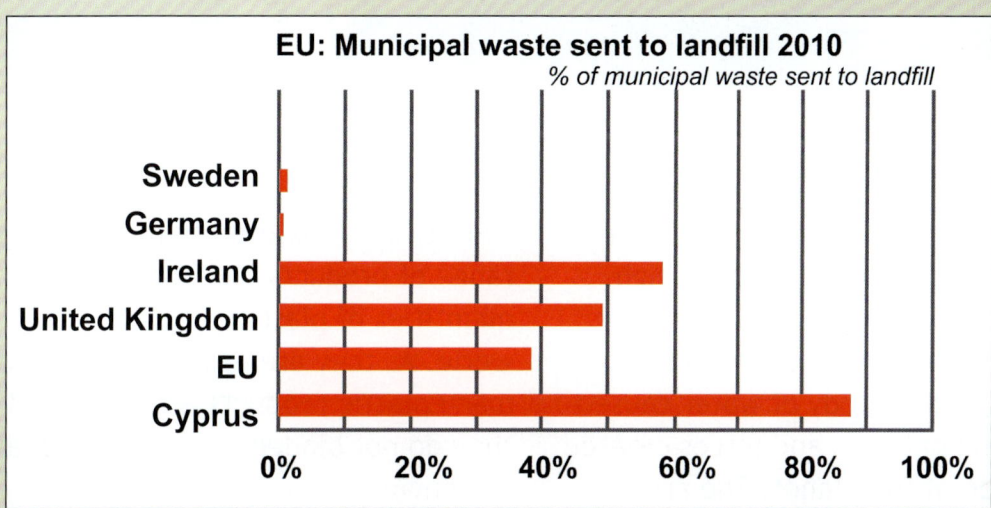

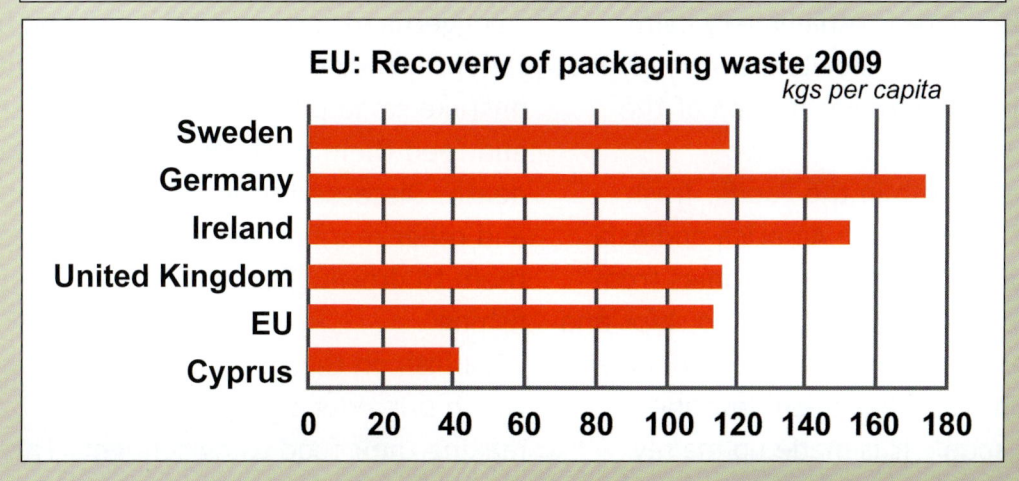

EU: Municipal waste generated 2010 (kgs per capita)
- Sweden: ~460
- Germany: ~580
- Ireland: ~610
- United Kingdom: ~520
- EU: ~500
- Cyprus: ~770

EU: Municipal waste sent to landfill 2010 (% of municipal waste sent to landfill)
- Sweden: ~1%
- Germany: ~1%
- Ireland: ~57%
- United Kingdom: ~49%
- EU: ~38%
- Cyprus: ~87%

EU: Recovery of packaging waste 2009 (kgs per capita)
- Sweden: ~115
- Germany: ~175
- Ireland: ~150
- United Kingdom: ~115
- EU: ~110
- Cyprus: ~40

1. From these graphs identify:
   (a) An area of waste management in which Ireland performs well.
   (b) An area of waste management in which Ireland performs badly.
   (c) An area of waste management in which Ireland could improve on.
2. Suggest an approach that could be used to improve Ireland's disposal and recycling of materials.
3. **Group work:** Find out what Sweden and Germany use instead of landfill to manage their waste.

Case Study: The Pacific Trash Vortex

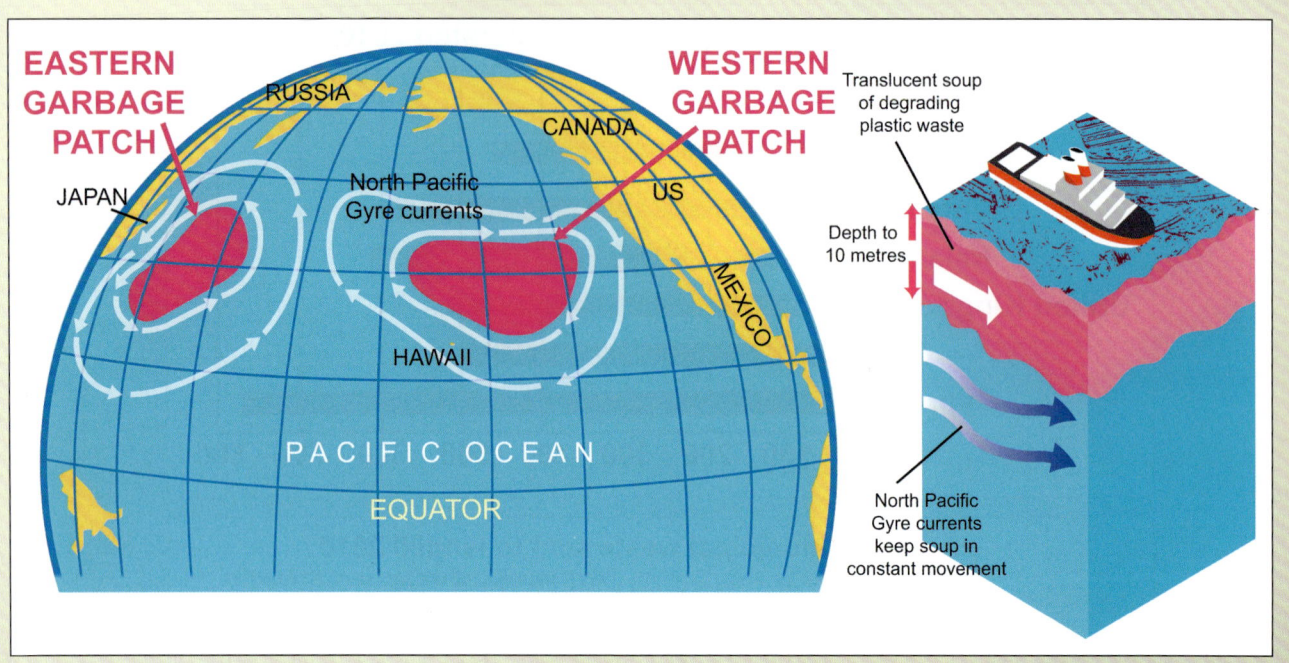

The Pacific Trash Vortex is a region in the North Pacific Ocean that contains a high density of plastic.

The vortex is an ocean gyre. A gyre is a large, slowly circling body of water caused by Earth's wind patterns and forces created by the rotation of the planet. The area in the centre of a gyre is usually very calm and stable. Rubbish is slowly drawn into this stable area by the circular motion of the currents.

Most of the rubbish in the Pacific Trash Vortex comes from North America and Asia. The other rubbish found there comes from boats, offshore oil rigs, large cargo ships and shipping containers that have been dumped.

This rubbish patch has been described as a 'plastic soup'. It is made up mainly of tiny bits of floating plastic called microplastics. Microplastics form when larger pieces of debris are broken down by sunlight. However, many larger pieces sink to the bottom of the Pacific Ocean, so the full extent of the debris has not yet been measured.

Plastics can be used to make a large range of products. For these reasons, huge quantities of plastic are used around the world. As they are easy and cheap to replace many plastic products are discarded and as they do not biodegrade plastic remains in the environment.

Loggerhead turtles mistake plastic bags for jellyfish, their favourite food. Albatrosses mistake small pieces of plastic for fish eggs and feed them to chicks which often causes death. Discarded fishing nets can trap seals and other marine mammals and cause them to drown. This is referred to as 'ghost fishing'.

Rubbish on the surface blocks sunlight which prevents algae and plankton from making their food using sunlight. This will disturb ocean food webs and reduce the fish stocks that humans rely on.

As plastics are broken up they give out harmful pollutants which have been linked to environmental and health problems. These chemicals enter the food chain when eaten by marine organisms, causing harm

Life Cycle of Materials — 26

to all the animals in ocean food webs and to the people who in turn eat contaminated food.

Cleaning up the Plastic Vortex

Cleaning up the vortex may be an impossible task and many campaign groups focus on reducing the use of plastics instead of clearing this rubbish patch. One problem with trying to clear the patch is the size of many of the particles. Their small size is similar to that of many small ocean creatures, so using nets would capture these creatures as well as the plastic.

Another question is, whose responsibility should it be? No one country is close to this area so no nation has taken responsibility to address or fund any clear-up. Since 2014 aerial drones have been used to carry out further research on the rubbish.

Questions

1. Explain where the Pacific Trash Vortex can be found on a world map.
2. The Pacific Trash Vortex is an ocean gyre. Explain what a gyre is.
3. When rubbish enters one of the ocean currents what part of the gyre is it slowly moved to?
4. What feature of plastic means that it is the most common material found in this trash vortex?
5. It is very difficult to get an exact measurement of the area of this trash vortex. Give two reasons why an accurate measurement has not been made.
6. What happens to plastic in sunlight?
7. List two negative environmental impacts that are a direct result of this rubbish.
8. What approach are environmental campaigners taking in response to this situation?

27 Measurements and Units

Review Questions

1. Name three units that are used to measure length. (a) _____
   (b) _____
   (c) _____
2. What are the units of mass? _____
3. Name an instrument that can be used to measure mass. _____
4. What units are used to measure volume? _____
5. Calculate the volume of the box shown below. _____

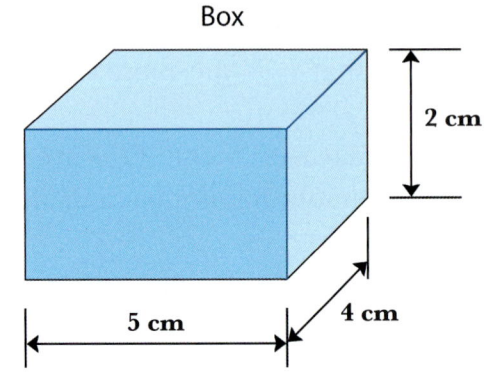

Box

2 cm
5 cm
4 cm

6. Name the instruments in the photographs below and give an example of what they could be used to measure:

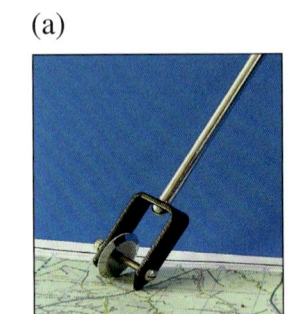

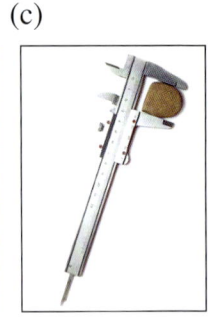

(a)   (b)   (c)

(a) _____
(b) _____
(c) _____

7. What instruments would you use to measure the following:
   (a) The length of a football pitch. _____
   (b) The volume of a small stone. _____
   (c) The diameter of a pencil. _____
   (d) The volume of a glass of milk. _____

Knowledge and Understanding

1. Calculate the area of the following rectangles.

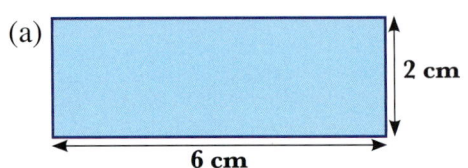

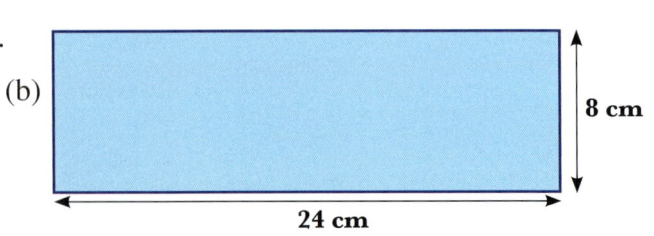

   (a) 2 cm × 6 cm

   (b) 8 cm × 24 cm

Measurements and Units 27

2. The diagram shows a leaf on a grid. Each square of the grid has an area of 1 cm².
   (a) Estimate the area of the leaf.
   (b) Explain how you made your estimate.

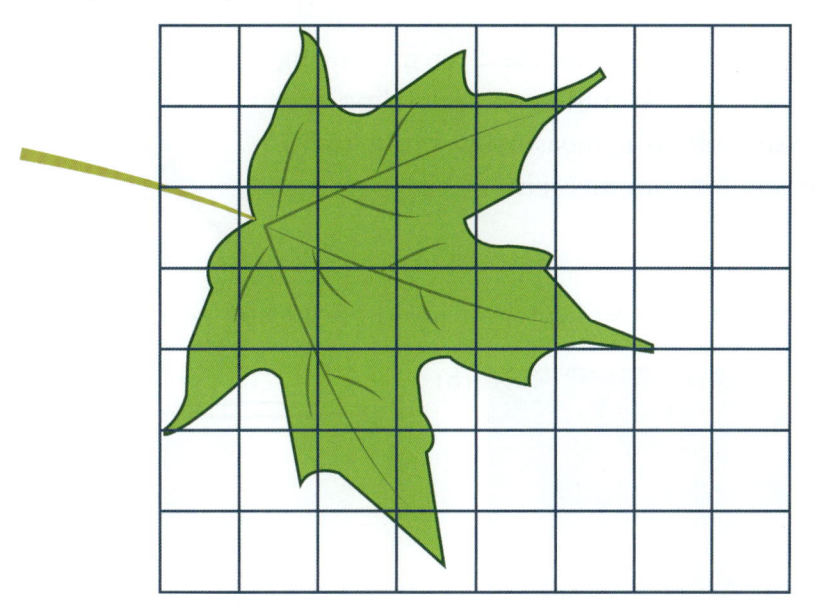

3. The picture shows two small objects beside a metal ruler.
   (a) Estimate the lengths of the sides of the objects shown. How could the accuracy of the measurement be improved using the metal ruler?
   (b) Name a different instrument that would give a more accurate measurement.
   (c) Object A is a cube, estimate the surface area of the cube.
   (d) Estimate the volume of A. Use suitable units for your calculations.

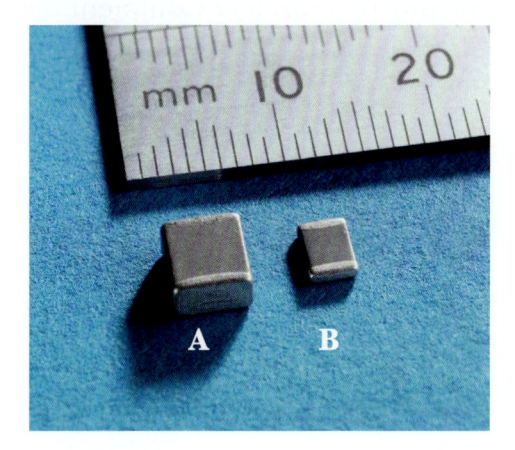

4. The diagrams below represent hits on a target made by four different people who were all aiming to hit the centre.

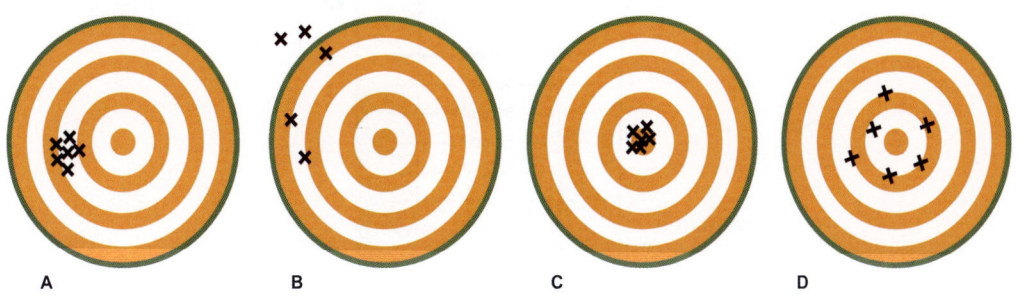

   A   B   C   D

   For each of the targets A, B, C and D comment on the **accuracy** and **precision** of the hits shown.

91

The Nature of Science Resources & Revision

5. The picture shows a clinical thermometer. Look carefully at the scale. Would this thermometer be suitable for measuring the boiling point of water? Give a reason for your answer.

   Clinical thermometers are normally used for measuring human body temperature. Would a school laboratory thermometer be suitable for measuring body temperature? Give a reason for your answer.

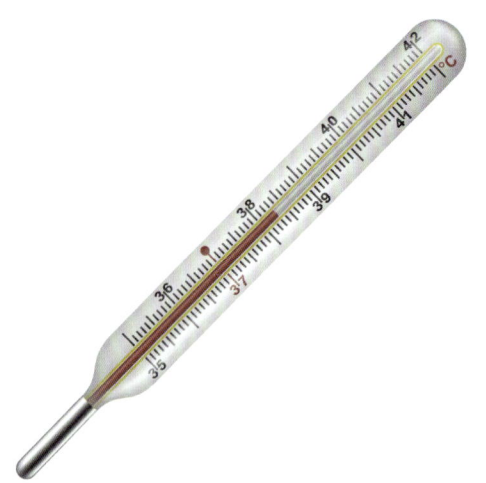

6. Which of the items below will give a more accurate reading for the volume of a liquid?

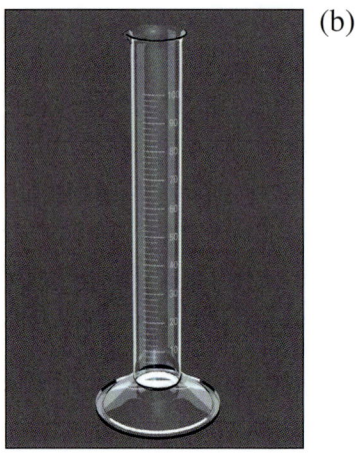

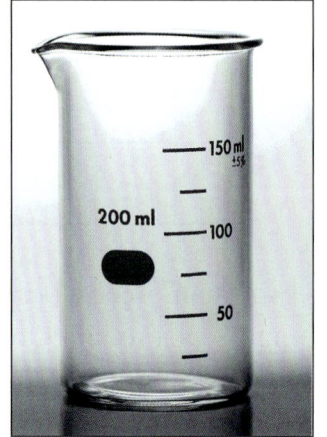

   (a)   (b)

7. The photograph below shows a section of a graduated cylinder containing some water. What is the volume of water in the measuring cylinder? Comment on the accuracy of the reading.

8. The diagram shows a measuring cylinder before (A) and after (B) a stone was added. What is the volume of the stone?

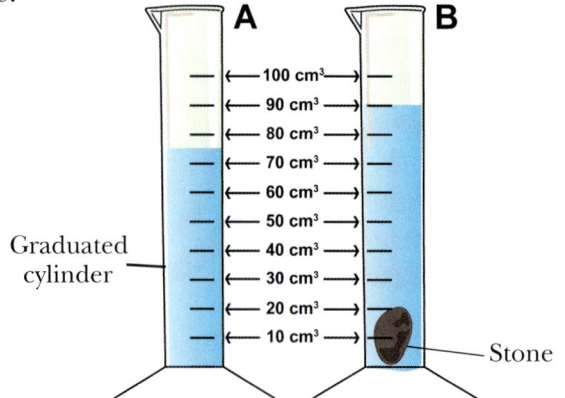

9. A class of students has been asked to measure the perimeter of their school playground. The students were divided into four groups and each group was given their own trundle wheel. Each group measured the perimeter of the playground four times and then worked out the average length. The results are shown below.

	Group 1	Group 2	Group 3	Group 4
Result 1	54.2	56.8	56.5	5.65
Result 2	54.2	55.9	56.6	56.3
Result 3	54.2	57.0	56.4	56.4
Result 4	54.1	56.2	56.5	56.2
Average	54.2	56.5	56.5	43.6375

Accuracy is how close a measured value is to the actual (true) value.
Precision is how close the measured values are to each other.

(a) The perimeter of the playground is actually 56.6 m. Which group made the most **accurate** measurements?
(b) Which group made the most **precise** measurements?
(c) Suggest why group 4 calculated a value that was much lower than the other groups.
(d) How might group 4 improve the accuracy of their overall result without taking any further measurements?
(e) Suggest a reason why the measurements of group 1 were less accurate than the measurements of group 3.
(f) One of the students in group 4 pointed out that their overall result went to 4 decimal places and concluded that their result was the most precise. Do you agree with this student? Give reasons for your answer.

10. A digital thermometer for home use has a display that shows temperature to the nearest $0.1°C$, but the instruction manual states that readings are only accurate to within $±0.2°C$. If the thermometer is used correctly and the actual body temperature being measured is $36.9°C$, what are the five possible values that could appear on the display?

28 Density, Speed and Acceleration

Review Questions

1. What is density? _____
   _____

2. What formula is used to calculate density? _____

3. What is the unit of density? _____

4. What is the density of water? _____

5. Explain why some substances float in liquids. _____
   _____

6. What is the density of a block of wood of volume 100 cm³ and mass 90 g? _____
   _____

7. What is speed? _____

8. What formula is used to calculate speed? _____

9. What is the difference between speed and velocity? _____
   _____

10. What is the unit of velocity? _____

11. What is acceleration? _____
    _____

12. What formula is used to calculate acceleration? _____

13. What is the unit of acceleration? _____

14. What is the difference between speed and acceleration? _____
    _____

Density, Speed and Acceleration   28

Knowledge and Understanding

1. Examine the table below showing the densities of different substances.

Substance	Ice	Alcohol	Wax	Wood
Density	0.93 g cm⁻³	0.87 g cm⁻³	0.72 g cm⁻³	0.64 g cm⁻³

   Draw a diagram to show what you would expect to happen if small pieces of (a) wood, (b) wax and (c) ice were placed in a beaker of alcohol.

2. The picture show a 'sky lantern' rising up in the air. Explain why lanterns rise when the flame is lit.

3. Describe, using a diagram in each case, how you would measure the density of the following: (a) an apple (b) engine oil.

4. The table to the right shows the densities of a variety of metals.
   (a) How have the metals in the table been arranged?

   (b) Rearrange the table so that the metals are listed in decreasing order of density.
   _____

Metal	Density (g cm⁻³)
Lead	11.3
Mercury	13.53
Nickel	8.9
Platinum	21.5
Potassium	0.89
Sodium	0.97
Water	1.0

   (c) What is the volume of 8 g of nickel?
   _____

   (d) What is the mass of 11 cm³ of platinum?
   _____

   (e) Which has a greater mass: 6 cm³ of mercury or 100 cm³ of potassium?
   _____

   (f) Which metals will sink in water?
   _____

   (g) Which metals will sink in mercury?
   _____

5. The density of candle wax is 0.72 g cm⁻³. A cylindrical candle has a radius of 2 cm and a height of 20 cm. Calculate the mass of the candle. (The volume of a cylinder is $\pi r^2 h$).

6. The mass of a beaker is 25.5 g when empty and 41.5 g when 20 cm³ of oil is placed in it.
   (a) What is the density of the oil?
   (b) Would this oil sink or float in water?

7. When an object is placed in water it floats; when placed in paraffin oil, it sinks.
   (a) What does this tell you about the object?
   (b) What might the object consist of?

8. The diagram shows a number of different liquids in a glass. The liquids have all got different densities.
   (a) Which liquid is the most dense?
   (b) Which liquid is the least dense?
   (c) The density of milk is 1.04 g cm⁻³ and the density of maple syrup is 1.3 g cm⁻³. Use this information to estimate the density of the dice, explaining how you made your estimate.
   (d) The density of surgical spirits is 0.87 g cm⁻³. What does this tell you about the density of the block of wood?
   (e) The density of steel is 8 g cm⁻³. What does this tell you about the density of honey?
   (f) What would you expect to observe if some water was carefully poured into the glass?

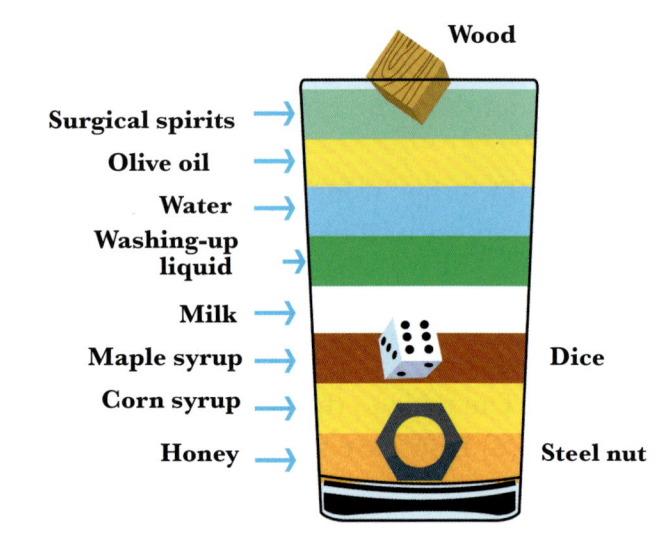

9. If a car travels 300 m in 12 seconds what is its average speed?
10. A car increases its velocity from 25 m s⁻¹ to 35 m s⁻¹ in 5 seconds. Calculate its acceleration.
11. The velocity of a car changes from 12 m s⁻¹ to 30 m s⁻¹ in 6 seconds. Calculate its acceleration.
12. A car travelling at 46 m s⁻¹ slows down to 22 m s⁻¹ in 6 seconds. Calculate its deceleration.
13. A car travelling at 65 m s⁻¹ takes 13 seconds to come to a stop. Calculate its deceleration.
14. A train starting from rest accelerates at 5 m s⁻² for 4 seconds. Calculate its velocity at the end of the 4 seconds.
15. A car starts from rest with a constant acceleration of 6 m s⁻². How long will it take to reach a speed of 48 m s⁻¹?
16. The table shows the distances travelled at different times by a girl running.

Time (s)	0	2	4	6	8	10	12	14	16
Distance (m)	0	6	12	18	24	30	36	42	48

(a) Graph the results, putting time on the horizontal (x) axis.
(b) Use the graph to find:
   (i) the time taken to run 15 metres
   (ii) the distance travelled in 11 seconds
   (iii) the speed of the runner

Density, Speed and Acceleration 28

(c) What does the shape of the graph tell you about the relationship between time and distance?
(d) Sketch a similar graph to represent the girl gradually speeding up as she runs.
(e) Sketch a similar graph to represent the girl gradually slowing down as she runs.

17. This table shows the velocity of a motorbike at different times.

Time (s)	0	1	2	3	4	5
Velocity (m s^{-1})	0	4	8	12	16	20

(a) Graph the results, putting time on the horizontal (x) axis.
(b) Use the graph to find:
 (i) the velocity at 2.5 seconds
 (ii) the time at which the velocity is 10 m s^{-1}
 (iii) the acceleration of the motorbike
 (iv) the time taken to change from 4 m s^{-1} to 14 m s^{-1}
(c) Is the velocity unchanging (steady)?
(d) Is the motorbike accelerating?
(e) If the motorbike is accelerating is the acceleration constant?
(f) Draw a similar graph to represent the motorbike accelerating for 5 seconds, then keeping a constant velocity for 5 seconds and finally coming to a stop in 5 seconds.

18. Match the distance/time graphs (a) - (d) with the descriptions of the relationships (i) - (iv).

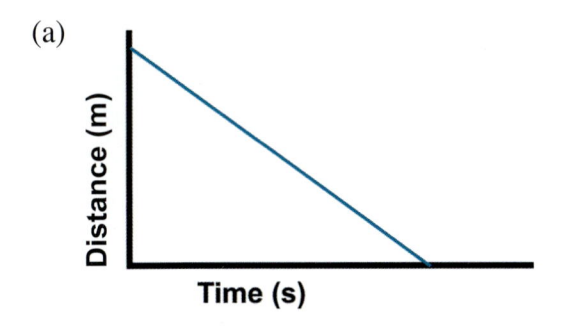

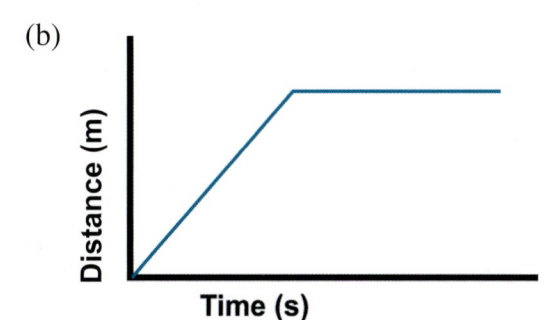

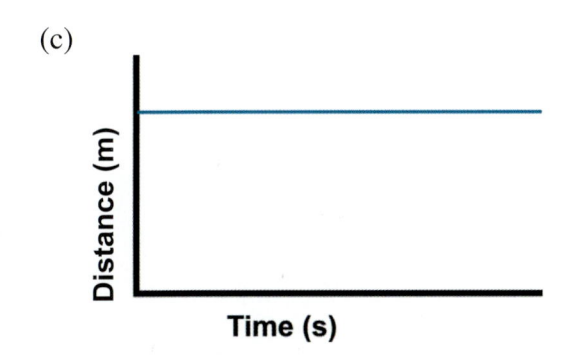

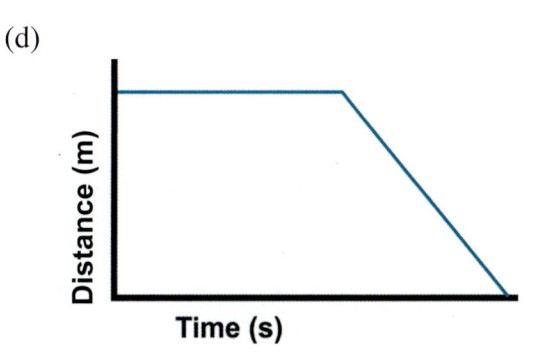

(i) As time increases, distance decreases.
(ii) As time increases, distance stays the same.
(iii) As time increases, distance stays the same for a while, and then decreases.
(iv) As time increases, distance increases for a while, and then stays the same.

19. Describe the relationship between **velocity** and **time** as shown in the following graphs (a) – (d).

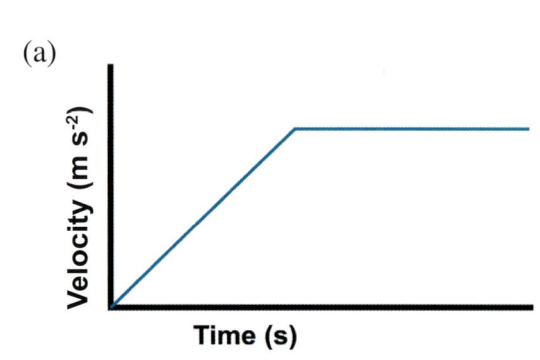

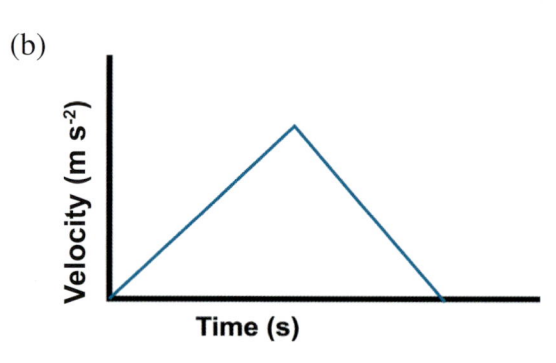

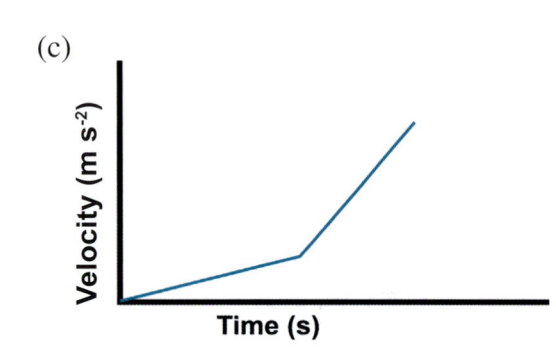

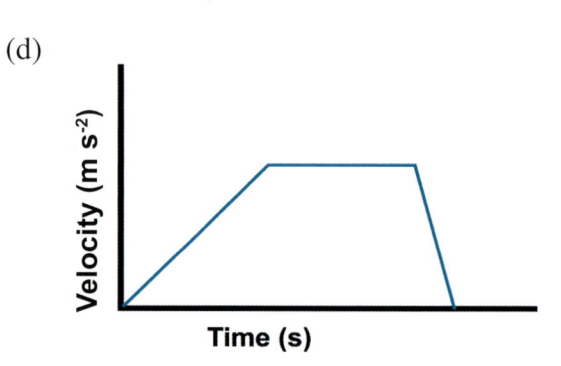

(a) Velocity (m s^{-2}) vs Time (s)

(b) Velocity (m s^{-2}) vs Time (s)

(c) Velocity (m s^{-2}) vs Time (s)

(d) Velocity (m s^{-2}) vs Time (s)

29 Force

Review Questions

1. List four types of force. For each type explain how it causes movement.
   (a) _____
   (b) _____
   (c) _____
   (d) _____

2. Which scientist developed the laws of motion? _____

3. How many laws of motion are there? _____

4. Which law of motion says that force is equal to mass times acceleration (F = ma)?
   _____

5. Which law of motion says that heavier objects require more force than lighter objects to move or accelerate them? _____

6. Which law says that for every action there is an equal and opposite reaction?
   _____

7. What is friction? _____
   _____

8. Give two advantages of friction.   (a) _____
                                       (b) _____

9. Give two disadvantages of friction. (a) _____
                                       (b) _____

The Nature of Science Resources & Revision

Knowledge and Understanding

Case Study Formula 1

A modern Formula 1 car has almost as much in common with a jet fighter as it does with an ordinary car. Aerodynamics (how an object interacts with the air) has become key to success in the sport, and teams spend tens of millions on research and development each year.

A car designer has two main concerns: to create downforce to help push the car's tyres down onto the track for good grip, and to minimise drag. Drag is caused by friction between the car and the air and it slows a car down. Downforce is created by using wings and spoilers mounted on the front and rear of the car. These cause the air to move more quickly across the underside of the spoiler. This means there is more air pressure above the spoiler than below. This pushes the car downwards. However these wings also cause drag. Engineers try to get the maximum downforce with the minimum drag.

Some cars even have electronically controlled wings so that the driver can increase the downforce on corners and reduce it on the straights.

It is not just the wings that are looked at however. Every single surface of a modern Formula 1 car, from the shape of the suspension links to that of the driver's helmet, has its aerodynamic effects considered. Look at a recent car and you will see that almost as much effort has been spent reducing drag as increasing downforce. They have smooth bodies made from one solid piece of carbon fibre. They are low and wide to allow the air to pass over them more easily. However the cars can't be too slippery as the air needs to be in contact with the car long enough to cool the engine.

A Formula 1 engine needs to be rebuilt after about 500 miles. Why? Because generating all of that power requires the engine to run very fast. Parts of the engine turn at nearly 19,000 revolutions per minute. Running an engine at such high rpms produces an enormous amount of friction which produces large amounts of heat and puts a great deal of stress on the moving parts. This is another reason why airflow is important. It cools the engine.

The tyres of a Formula 1 race car may be the most important part of the entire vehicle. They are the contact point between the car and the track. If they don't work well, the car won't perform well. Some tyres are called 'slick tyres'. These have no tread pattern so the entire tyre is in contact with the track. The tyres become extremely hot during the race which makes them softer, giving better grip. They work well in dry conditions but can skid easily in wet weather. Tyres with grooves in them are used on wet tracks as these are less likely to skid due to the uneven tyre surface. All Formula 1 car tyres are wide to give more contact with the ground.

sportstechnology.blogspot.ie (adapted)

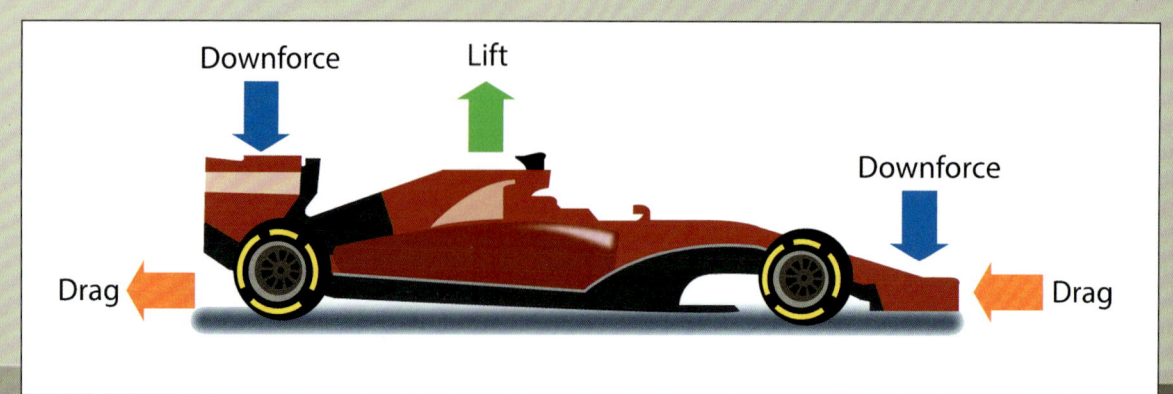

Questions

1. What is meant by aerodynamics?
2. What two forces are engineers concerned with in the design of Formula 1 cars?
3. How does a wing (or spoiler) affect the forces on a Formula 1 car?
4. What design features of the car reduce friction with the air?
5. There needs to be a high level of friction between the tyres and the road in order for the car to move. What factors are considered in the design of tyres of Formula 1 cars?
6. Where is friction an advantage in the design of a Formula 1 car?
7. Where is friction a disadvantage in the design of a Formula 1 car?

Analyse and Interpret

1. A pupil used the apparatus shown in the diagram to investigate the relationship between the force applied and the extension produced in the spring by that force. A pointer was used to read the scale. Weights were added to the pan to apply forces to the spring. The data recorded is in the table.

   (a) Calculate the **total** extension for each force and enter them in the table.

Force (N)	Metre stick value (cm)	Extension (cm) (extension = value - 31)
0	31.0	0
2	35.0	
4	39.0	
6	43.0	
8	47.0	
10	51.0	

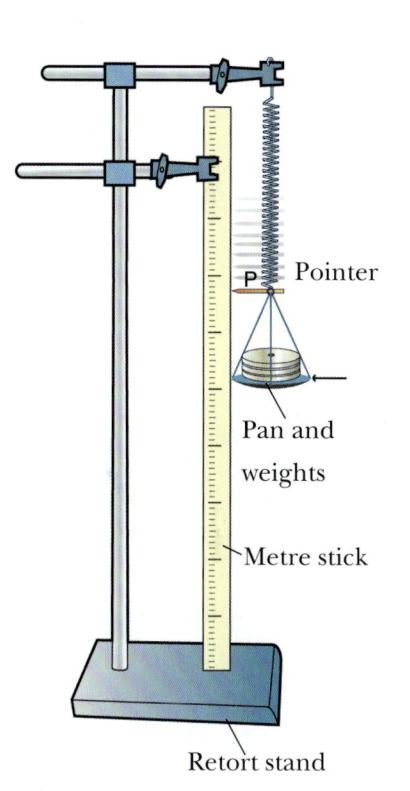

(b) Draw a graph of force against total extension in the grid below.

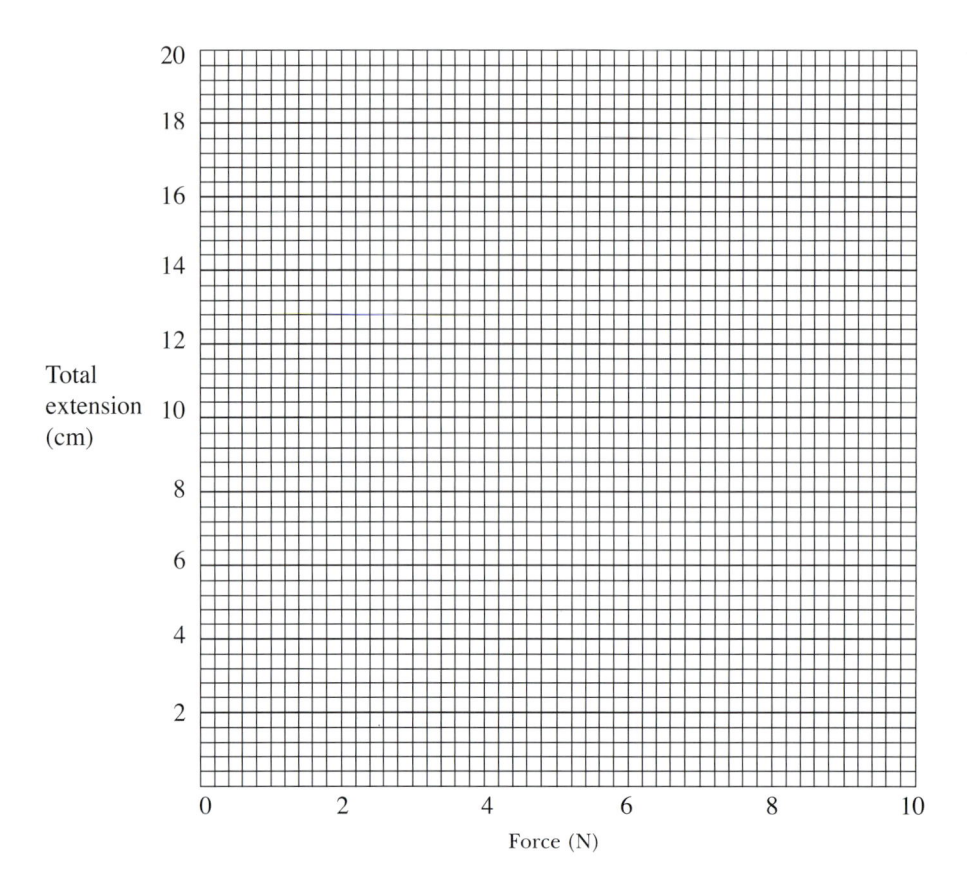

Total extension (cm) vs Force (N)

(c) What conclusion can be drawn from the graph regarding the relationship between the force applied to the spring and the extension produced by it?

(d) Use the graph to determine the weight of a stone that produced an extension of 14 cm in the spring.

2. The picture shows an apple falling and a feather falling inside a vacuum tube. Each image of the apple and the feather is taken at 0.05 second intervals.

   (a) Do the apple and feather fall at the same rate?
   (b) If you repeated this experiment in the classroom without a vacuum tube would you see the same result? Explain your answer.
   (c) Why do the gaps between the pictures of the apple appear to get bigger as the apple falls?
   (d) How could you use this method to calculate acceleration due to gravity?

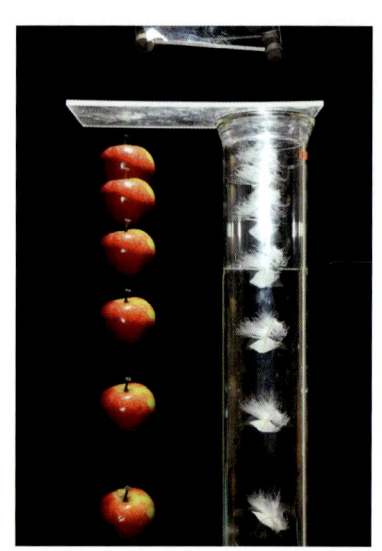

30 Energy

Review Questions

1. What is energy? _____

2. What units are used to measure energy? _____

3. Identify Earth's primary source of energy. _____

4. The natural process that captures light energy from the sun and converts it into chemical energy in food is called _____ .

5. The process that occurs in cells and releases energy from food is called _____ .

6. Identify the type(s) of energy found in each of the following:
   (a) A potato _____
   (b) A glowing light bulb _____
   (c) A child sitting at the top of a slide _____
   (d) A stretched elastic band _____
   (e) A wire connecting an appliance to a socket that has been switched on _____
   (f) The nucleus of an atom _____
   (g) A flame _____
   (h) A banging drum _____
   (i) A wheel rolling along a road _____

7. The law of conservation of energy states that energy cannot be _____ or _____, it can only change from _____ _____ into another.

Knowledge and Understanding

1. The sun is the primary source of energy for Earth. Explain what is meant by 'primary source of energy'.
2. Plants are able to use the sun's energy directly. How do plants (a) provide energy for animals and (b) form fuels?

The Nature of Science Resources & Revision

3. Fill in the energy input and one output in the following devices.

(a)
Energy input: _____
Energy output: _____

(b)
Energy input: _____
Energy output: _____

(c)
Energy input: _____
Energy output: _____

(d)
Energy input: _____
Energy output: _____

(e)
Energy input: _____
Energy output: _____

(f)
Energy input: _____
Energy output: _____

(g)
Energy input: _____
Energy output: _____

(h)
Energy input: _____
Energy output: _____

(i)
Energy input: _____
Energy output: _____

4. When a child is pushed on a swing he/she will swing up and down a certain number of times and eventually come to a stop. Explain what is happening in terms of energy changes and energy dissipation.

Energy 30

5. This Sankey diagram represents the energy input and output of a desk lamp.

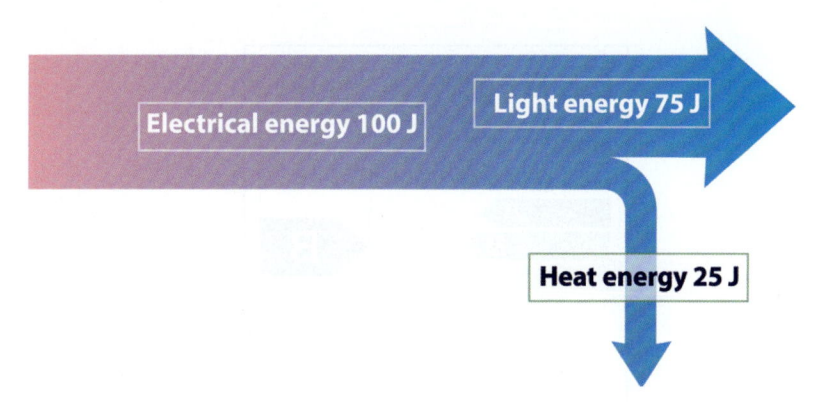

Electrical energy 100 J → **Light energy 75 J**
↓ **Heat energy 25 J**

(a) How much of the output energy is useful energy?
(b) How much of the output energy is dissipated?
(c) Calculate the efficiency of the lamp.

6. Calculate the % efficiency of the devices listed in the table, using the following formula:

$$\frac{\text{Useful energy output (J)}}{\text{Total energy input (J)}} \times 100 = \text{\% Efficiency}$$

Device	Energy input	Energy output	Efficiency
Food processor	450 J	Useful energy 225 J Dissipated energy 225 J	
TV	2000 J	Useful energy 1350 J Dissipated energy 650 J	
MP3 player	270 J	Useful energy 225 J Dissipated energy 45 J	
Tumble dryer	3500 J	Useful energy 2450 J Dissipated energy 1050 J	
Games console	2000 J	Useful energy 1600 J Dissipated energy 400 J	
Mobile phone	150 J	Useful energy 102 J Dissipated energy 48 J	

7. The average dishwasher does 250 washes per year. An energy-efficient dishwasher could save a household €12 per year on their electricity bill compared with a less energy-efficient model. The more energy-efficient model costs €60 more than the less energy-efficient model. How long will it take for the household to benefit from the yearly savings of using an energy-efficient dishwasher?

8. A family buys a fridge freezer with the following energy-efficiency label. What does this label tell the customer about the appliance?

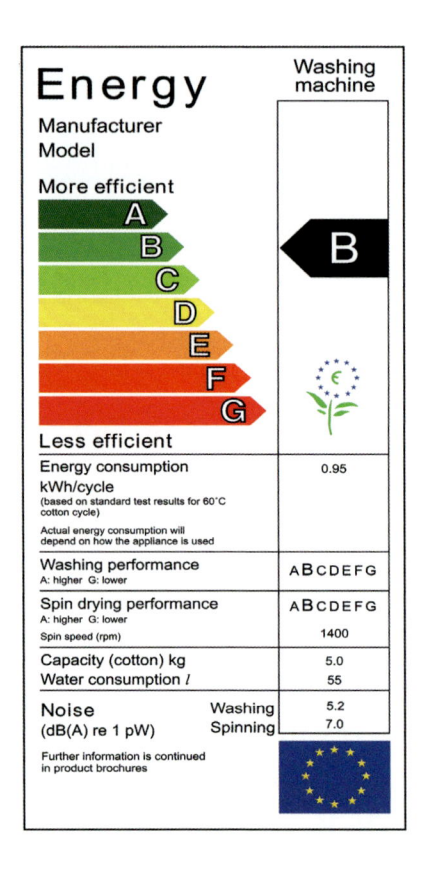

9. The chain of a bicycle has become rusty. A lot of motion energy is lost to friction when the cyclist is pushing the pedals. How could the efficiency of the bicycle be improved?

10. Design a poster to make people aware of how they can make their homes more energy efficient.

31 Electricity

Review Questions

1. List the particles present in an atom. _____

2. Which particles are in the nucleus? _____

3. Where are the other particles? _____

4. What charge do each of these particles have? _____

5. Which of these particles can be added to or removed from an atom? _____

6. How does an atom become charged? _____

7. State the overall charge of each of the following objects.

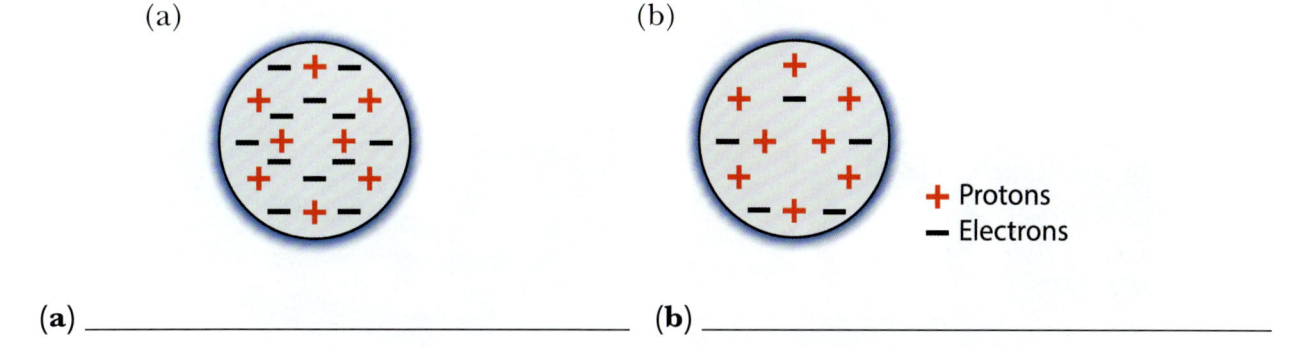

(a) (b)

+ Protons
− Electrons

(a) _____ (b) _____

Knowledge and Understanding

1. When a ruler is rubbed with a nylon cloth, electrons are transferred from the cloth to the ruler. Explain why the ruler is now able to pick up small pieces of paper.

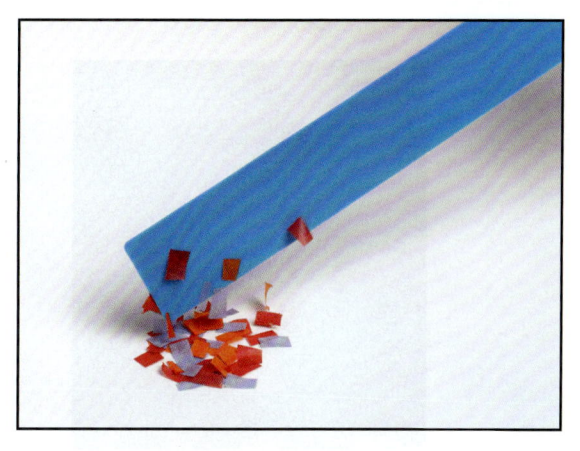

2. What type of electricity is illustrated in the example above?

107

3. What is the difference between static electricity and current electricity?
4. The picture below shows a circuit containing a paper clip. The bulb lights up when the paper clip is connected to the circuit. Which of the items labelled (i) – (iii) (biro, tinfoil, cord) will enable the bulb to light when connected to the circuit? Explain your answer.

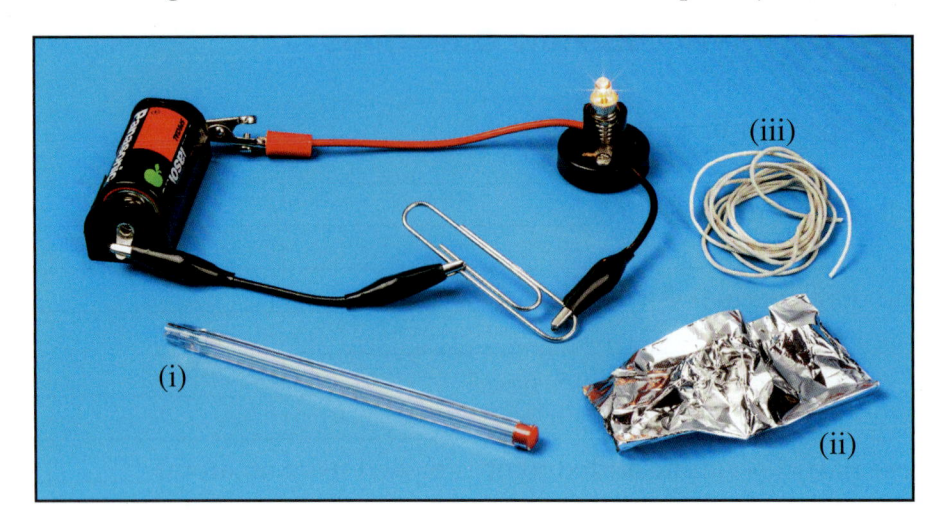

5. What is the unit of electric current?
6. Which of these instruments (A or B) can be used to measure electric current?

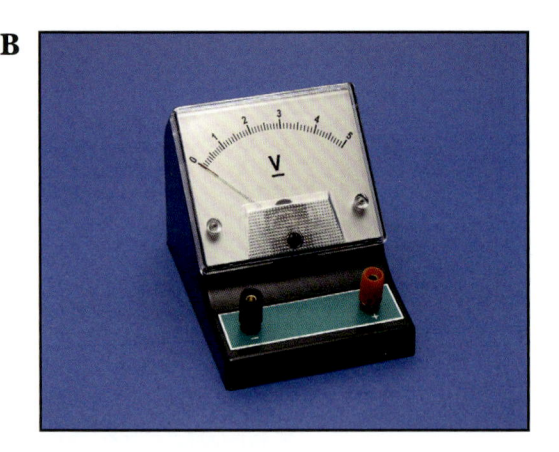

7. Potential difference is the difference in electrical potential between two points in a circuit. What is the unit of potential difference?
8. When an electric current flows through a circuit containing a filament light bulb the particles of the filament oppose the flow of electrons. (a) What is this called? (b) Why does the bulb light up?

9. What is the unit and symbol of electrical resistance?

Electricity 31

10. What is the current in this circuit?

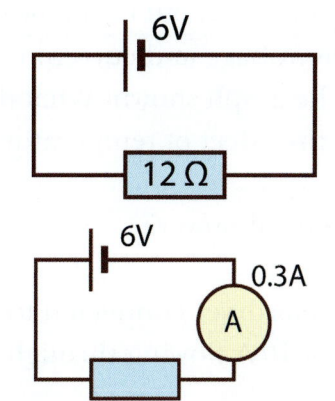

11. What is the resistance in this circuit?

12. The diagram shows an experiment set up to investigate Ohm's Law.

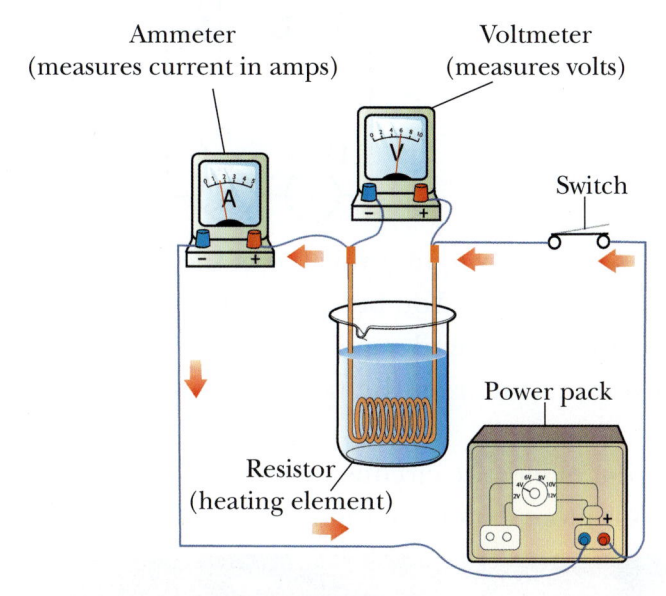

The following measurements were recorded

Voltage (V)	Current (A)
2	0.4
4	0.8
6	1.2
8	1.6
10	2.0

(a) Draw a line graph to represent this data (current on *x*-axis and voltage on *y*-axis).
(b) What is the resistance of the heating element?
(c) Use your graph to find the current passing through the circuit when the voltage is 9 V.
(d) Use your graph to find the voltage across the heating element when the current passing through is 1.0 A.
(e) What does your graph tell you about the relationship between current and voltage?
(f) Why is the heating element placed in water?

(g) The heating element was taken out of the beaker and began to heat up. The voltage and current measurements collected produced the graph shown. What does this graph tell you about the effect of temperature on Ohm's Law?

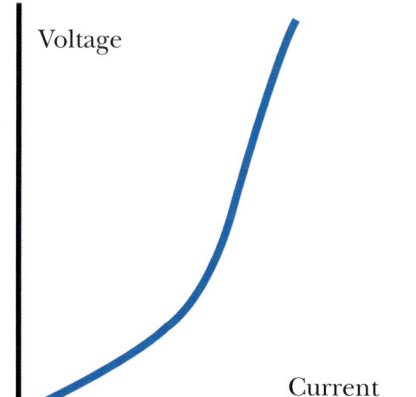

13. What is the unit of electrical power?

14. What is the power of a hairdryer connected to a 12 V battery with a current of 10 A flowing through it?

15. What is the current flowing through a radio that is connected to a 12 V battery and has a power of 72 W?

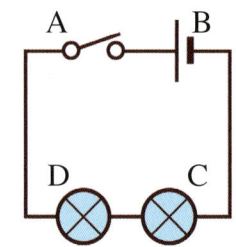

16. List the components A-D in this circuit.

17. At Christmas there are two sets of fairy lights available in the shop.
Set A costs €24.95 and set B costs €4.95. You buy set A and your friend buys set B.
On the way home both you and your friend manage to crush one of the bulbs on each of your sets of fairy lights. When you put them on the tree later your set lights up but your friend's set does not.
 (a) Using your understanding of electric circuits explain why this has happened.
 (b) Why do you think set A is more expensive than set B?

18. What type of electric circuit do you think is used in the headlights of a car? Explain your answer.

32 Electronics

Review Questions

1. What is the symbol for a resistor? _____

2. What unit is resistance measured in? _____

3. What happens to the resistance of a light dependent resistor (LDR) when a bright light is shone directly at it? _____
_____

4. For each of the resistors shown in Fig. 1, calculate the resistance using the code given in Fig. 2.
    (a) _____
    (b) _____
    (c) _____
    (d) _____
    (e) _____

Fig. 1

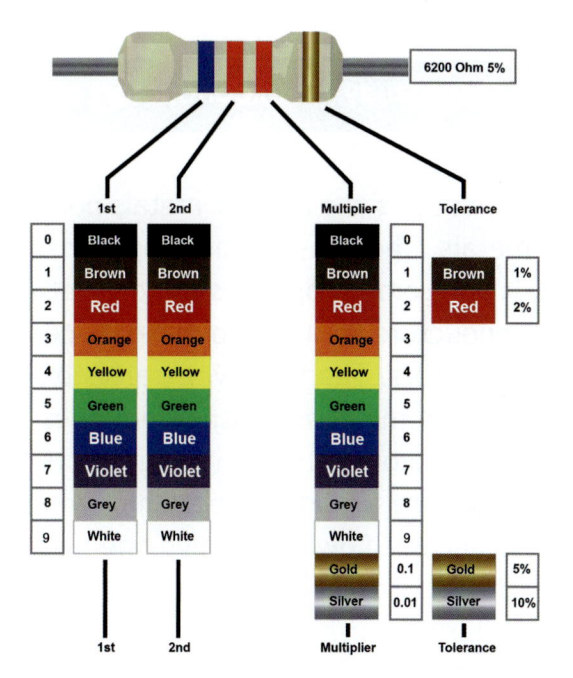

Fig. 2

5. What is the symbol for a diode? _____

The Nature of Science Resources & Revision

6. Draw a circuit in the box below showing a diode in forward bias.

7. What advantages have LEDs over light bulbs?
_____
_____

Knowledge and Understanding

Case Study   Semiconductors and the world of computers

Semiconductors are neither metals nor non-metals. They have some properties of metals and some properties of non-metals. Semiconductors are used to make diodes and transistors. The first ever transistor was made from paper clips, razorblades and the semiconductor germanium in 1947. Transistors are a kind of electronic switch. A small current flowing through one part (called the base) lets the transistor allow a much larger current to flow in the main circuit. This means that if there is a current, even a very small one, through the base the transistor is said to be switched on. If there is no current flowing in the base then the transistor is said to be switched off. Transistors therefore have two settings: on or off. The 'on' setting is given the number 1 and the 'off' setting is given the number 0. Long series of transistors set to 1 or 0 give many possible combinations. This is the basis of the binary language used in computer coding. Each transistor, or digit, is called a bit. Eight transistors set to combinations of 'off' and 'on' make up a byte. Bytes make up gigabytes and terabytes which we tend to use to compare the processing power of computers. At the Intel fabrication plant in Leixlip, Co. Kildare the semiconductor silicon is used to make computer processors, the most recent of which contain 1.4 million transistors. Silicon is the second most common element on earth (after oxygen) and is collected from grains of sand. It could be said that the processors in your telephone, your computer, your calculator and all other electronic devices you use every day are made from sand! Scientists are constantly working to make transistors and other electronic components as small as possible. We call this branch of science, nanoscience.

Electronics 32

Questions
1. What makes semiconductors so useful in electronic circuits?
2. Name two semiconductors.
3. What is the main electronic component in computer processors?
4. What switches a transistor on or off?
5. What binary digit is given to a transistor when it is on?
6. What binary digit is given to a transistor when it is off?
7. One transistor can have a binary digit of 1 or 0; two transistors can give a code of 00; 01; 10 or 11. How many combinations can three transistors make?
8. How many transistors do modern computer processors contain?
9. Why do you think scientists are always trying to make components smaller?

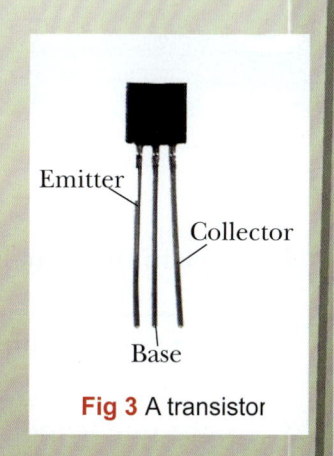

Fig 3 A transistor

Analyse and Interpret

The table below shows the results of an experiment carried out to investigate the effect of light on the resistance of an LDR.

Distance between LDR and light source (cm)	Resistance (ohms)
10	160
20	310
30	405
40	470
50	500
60	525
70	540
80	550
90	556
100	558

1. Draw a graph of the results. Label both axes clearly and select an appropriate scale.
2. What general relationship does the graph show between distance from light source and resistance?
3. Are distance and resistance directly proportional? Explain your answer.
4. Suggest a reason why moving the light source from 90 cm away from the LDR to 100 cm away makes less of a difference than moving the light source from 20 cm away from the LDR to 30 cm away?

33 Technology in Our Lives

Review Questions

1. Explain the term technology. _____
   _____

2. Apart from communication what other activities use technology? _____
   _____

3. Name one school activity that uses technology and give the advantage of using that technology.
   _____
   _____

4. Identify four technologies that help to make life in your community safer.
   (a) _____ (c) _____
   (b) _____ (d) _____

5. List six tasks that both smartphones and computers can perform.
   (a) _____ (d) _____
   (b) _____ (e) _____
   (c) _____ (f) _____

Knowledge and Understanding

Case Study   Developments in solar cells

Breakthrough in solar panel manufacture promises cheap energy within a decade

A breakthrough in the production of solar cells will make solar panels cheaper and safer, and solar energy will develop quickly over the next decade, scientists said.

A technical advance using an edible salt could revolutionise the production of future solar panels to make them less expensive and easier to use than the current models.

Researchers believe they have found a way of overcoming one of the most serious difficulties of the latest type of solar panel, which is based on toxic cadmium chloride, by simply adding magnesium chloride, an abundant salt found in seawater.

A study has shown that the solar cells produced with magnesium chloride work just as efficiently as those produced using cadmium chloride but at a fraction of the cost and with much lower toxicity.

'We believe it's going to make a big change to the costs of these devices. The cost of solar is going to match fossil fuels eventually but this is going to get us there quicker,' said Dr Jon Major of the University of Liverpool, who led the research. 'Magnesium chloride is incredibly low-cost and it is simply recovered from seawater. It is used to de-ice roads in winter and it is completely harmless and non-toxic. We've managed to replace a highly expensive, toxic material with one that's safe and low-cost.'

About 90 per cent of the solar panels currently in use are made of photovoltaic cells composed of silicon semiconductors. These convert sunlight directly into electricity. However, silicon is not good at absorbing sunlight which is why more efficient photovoltaic cells have been developed using a thin coating of cadmium telluride, which absorbs sunlight so well that it only needs to be about one hundredth of the thickness of silicon.

However, although cadmium telluride is seen as the future for solar energy, it is 'activated' with toxic cadmium chloride to raise its efficiency of converting sunlight to electricity from about two per cent to 15 per cent or more.

The Liverpool team tried to find an alternative to cadmium chloride in the activation step and discovered that it could be done just as well with magnesium chloride. In a study published in the journal *Nature*, researchers demonstrated that the efficiency of the photovoltaic cells made from cadmium telluride and magnesium chloride were equal to commercial cadmium telluride cells that had been activated with toxic cadmium chloride.

'Magnesium chloride is about one per cent of the cost of cadmium chloride. In addition, waste disposal will be far easier and cheaper with a product based on a non-toxic salt,' Dr Major said.

The development is exciting because it promises to make the industry even more competitive with conventional sources of energy, such as fossil fuels.

The Independent (adapted)

Questions
1. What discovery is discussed in this article?
2. What advantage does it have over the use of cadmium chloride?
3. How will technology using this discovery help humans to use energy more sustainably?
4. This material will allow solar panels to be made more cheaply. Discuss the impact of this on future use of solar energy.

Case Study: Technology and the Irish emergency services

TETRA Ireland is the company that provides the digital radio network that is used by An Garda Síochána, the ambulance and fire services, Irish Coast Guard, health agencies and the military. This network was purpose-built to meet the needs of these services.

Technological requirements of the emergency services

The emergency services needed several features for an effective communication system. These included secure, private communication, the ability to interact with one or more services at the same time and a reliable network with coverage across all areas which would work regardless of power outages, weather conditions and sabotage.

Resulting system

A reliable and resilient communications system was built to allow information sharing among the different services as part of an overall response to an emergency.

System effectiveness

A reliable radio system makes search and rescue communication more secure and effective and helps to keep rescue personnel and the people that they are rescuing safe.

The Irish Coast Guard reported that by using TETRA, their Rescue Co-ordinaton Centres can alert helicopter crew pilots, winchmen, winch operators and engineers all on one call. And as they make their way to the airfield, updates on the preparedness of the helicopter are also given. An additional advantage is that the system allows direct communication between the Rescue Co-ordination Centre and rescue personnel, such as a helicopter winchman dropped into a remote mountain area.

Questions

1. Identify the problem that this technology was used to solve.
2. How does this system meet the requirements of the emergency services?
3. Give an advantage of using this technology instead of relying on mobile phone communication.
4. If someone in your family worked in one of these services explain why you might feel reassured about their safety knowing that this communication system is used.
5. Would you say that this technology has any of these impacts: scientific, societal or environmental? Explain your answer.

34 Generating Electricity

Review Questions

1. List three ways that the electricity we use can be generated.
   (a) _____ (b) _____ (c) _____

2. Explain the term ethical.
   _____

3. Explain the term unethical.
   _____

4. What is an ethical issue?
   _____

5. When evaluating an energy source its sustainability must be considered. What does 'sustainability' mean?
   _____

6. Fill in the missing words from this diagram showing the three pillars of sustainability.

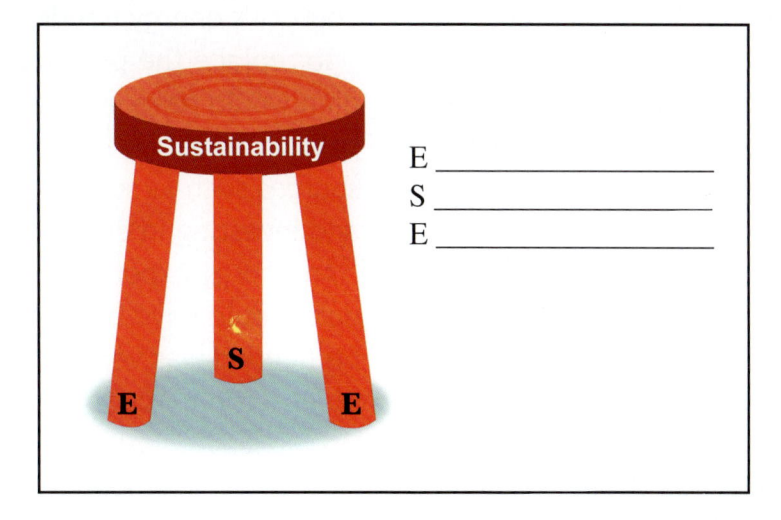

   E _____
   S _____
   E _____

7. Outline what each of the three pillars of sustainability mean.
   (a) _____
   (b) _____
   (c) _____

Knowledge and Understanding

Case Study: Generating electricity from hydroelectric power

The Baker River flows through a rugged landscape in Patagonia, Chile.

Chile's government cancelled a controversial plan for five hydroelectric dams on two of Patagonia's wildest rivers, after an eight-year battle between environmentalists and developers.

The HidroAysén project would have put hydroelectric dams on two rivers, causing flooding in 5,900 hectares of land.

The project had previously been approved but there was strong public opposition to the plan. Opponents stated that 'These giant dams would have put at risk the wilderness, traditional culture and local tourism economy of this remarkable region.'

In recent years Chile has struggled to provide energy for its growing economy. The country has few fossil fuel resources. The dams would have provided 15 to 20% of the country's energy needs.

To replace the power that the cancelled dam would have generated, the government plan on investing in other renewable energy sources such as solar and geothermal energy, and investing in energy efficiency.

An energy expert told reporters that the dam would have been efficient. 'The area to be flooded was very small for the amount of electricity it would have generated.'

National Geographic (adapted)

Generating Electricity 34

Questions

1. How many dams did Chile's government plan to build in Patagonia?
2. What area of land would have been flooded by the construction of the HidroAysén project dams?
3. Why do you think environmentalists opposed this project?
4. Why has Chile struggled to provide energy for its economy?
5. What percentage of the country's energy needs would have been met by these hydroelectric dams?
6. How does the government plan to replace the power that the cancelled dams would have generated?
7. Are hydroelectric dams a renewable or non-renewable source of energy?
8. What are the advantages of using a hydroelectric dam to generate electricity instead of burning fossil fuels in a power plant?
9. Based on the information contained in this article, do you think using the HidroAysén dams to generate electricity would have been (a) environmentally sustainable, (b) socially sustainable and (c) economically sustainable?
10. Do you think it would have been ethical for the HidroAysén project to go ahead? Justify your answer.

Read the sentences 1 – 6 below and answer the questions which follow.

1. Sean turns off the lights and closes the door when he leaves the room. He uses CFL light bulbs in all his light fittings.

2. Kayleigh leaves her laptop computer and mobile phone charging even when the battery is full. She leaves the TV and games console on standby all the time.

3. Lucy unplugs all her electrical devices after she has used them. She puts on an extra sweater when she is feeling cold instead of turning up the heating.

4. Peter turns on the dishwasher and washing machine every evening, even if they are only half full. He dries his clothes in the tumble dryer even if it is warm and sunny outside.

5. Sarah has a hot bath at night and turns on her electric blanket for two hours before she goes to bed at night.

6. Mia bought a new fridge with an A energy rating and she insulated the walls and attic in her house.

Questions

(a) Identify the energy conscious people in the list.

(b) Who is wasting electricity?

(c) How could they reduce their electricity consumption?

(d) Why is it important to be energy efficient and not waste electricity?

Analyse and Interpret

The following graph shows electricity consumption and the corresponding CO_2 production over a period of 24 hours in Ireland.

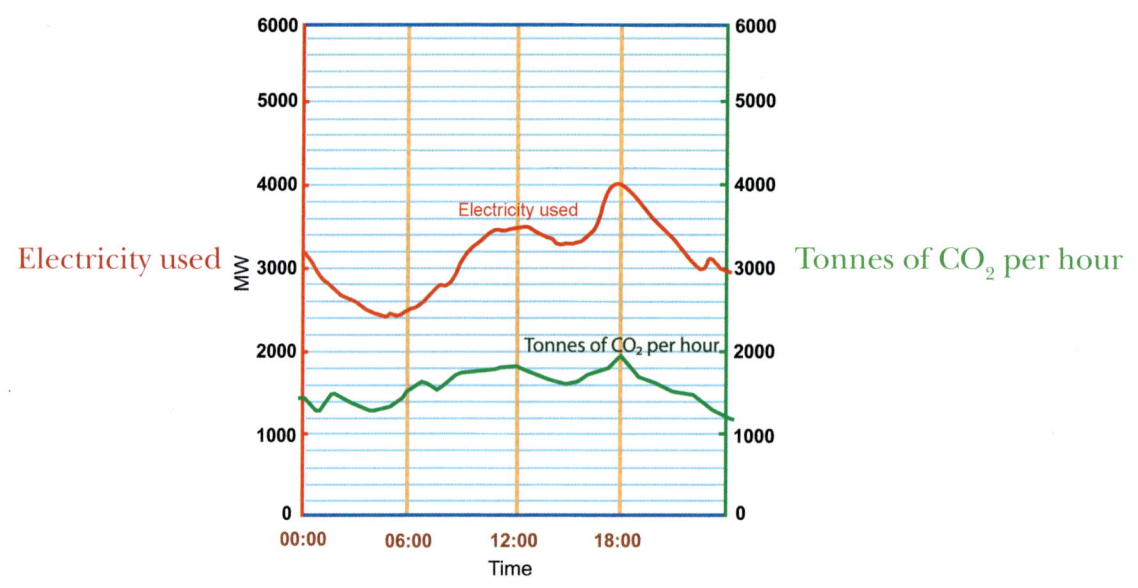

Fig. 9 The amount of electricity used in Ireland in a day and the resulting amount of CO_2 generated.

1. When is the demand for electricity lowest in the 24-hour time period?
2. Why do you think this is the case?
3. What time would you call 'peak demand'?
4. Why do you think demand is so high at this time?
5. What time period has the lowest CO_2 emissions?
6. Why do you think CO_2 emissions are at the lowest level at this time?
7. When are CO_2 emissions at the highest level?
8. Why do you think CO_2 emissions are at the highest level at this time?
9. What do these graphs tell you about the relationship between electricity consumption and CO_2 emissions?
10. What effect does an increase in CO_2 emissions have on Earth?

35 Our Universe

Review Questions

1. What is the universe?

2. (a) What is a star?

   (b) The planet Venus is sometimes called the 'Morning Star' because it can often be seen shining in the morning sky. Outline the differences between Venus and a star. Explain why people may wrongly consider Venus to be a star.

3. In what way is the orbit of a planet different to the orbit of other space objects such as asteroids?

4. Explain the difference between a planet and a dwarf planet.

5. What is a satellite?

6. What is the name of Earth's natural satellite? _____

7. Give one use for artificial satellites.

8. What term is used to describe a small object composed of frozen ice and gas that can glow and produce a tail? _____

9. Explain the difference between a solar system and a galaxy by giving a description of each.

10. What is gravity?

11. Outline the role of gravity in the formation of a solar system.

The Nature of Science Resources & Revision

12. Match each term **A–E** with the correct description **1–5** below:

    A. Planet   **1.** Earth's natural satellite   **A.** = ____
    B. Moon   **2.** Emits light   **B.** = ____
    C. Star   **3.** Much of its surface is covered with water   **C.** = ____
    D. Earth   **4.** Has a tail consisting of gas and dust   **D.** = ____
    E. Comet   **5.** Orbits stars and reflects light.   **E.** = ____

13. What is a comet's tail composed of? _____

14. What happens to a comet as it approaches the sun?
    _____

Knowledge and Understanding

1. Halley's Comet, shown in the photo, is a particularly bright comet which regularly orbits the sun. It was last seen in June 1986. The dates for the last five sightings of Halley's Comet are: 1986, 1910, 1835, 1759, 1682.
   Do you think the next sighting is more likely to occur in 2061 or 2071? Give reasons for your answer.

2. Place the following in order of size: star, galaxy, planet, solar system.

3. The photo shows a space object which is no bigger than a few kilometres in width.
   What evidence from the image suggests that this is an asteroid and not a dwarf planet?

4. The point at which an orbit is closest to the sun is called the **perihelion** and the point at which it is furthest away from the sun is called the **aphelion**.

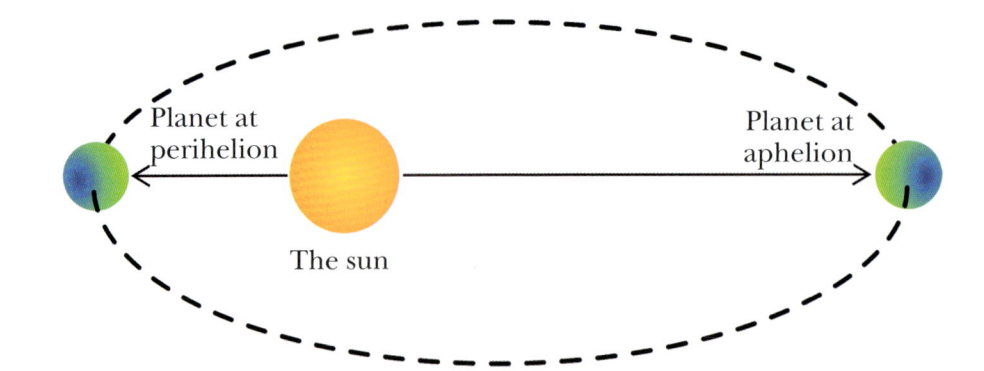

   Planet at perihelion   The sun   Planet at aphelion

Our Universe 35

	Neptune	**Pluto**
Perihelion (10^6 km)	4,444	4,435
Aphelion (10^6 km)	4,545	7,304

The table above gives details about the orbits of the planet Neptune and the dwarf planet Pluto.

(a) Which space object – Neptune or Pluto – moves closest to the sun during its orbit?

(b) Which space object – Neptune or Pluto – moves furthest away from the sun during its orbit?

(c) What is the difference between the perihelion and aphelion for (i) Neptune and (ii) Pluto?

(d) Which of the two space objects do you think has an orbit most like a circle? Give a reason for your answer.

(e) Which of the two space objects do you think has an orbit most like an elipse? Give a reason for your answer.

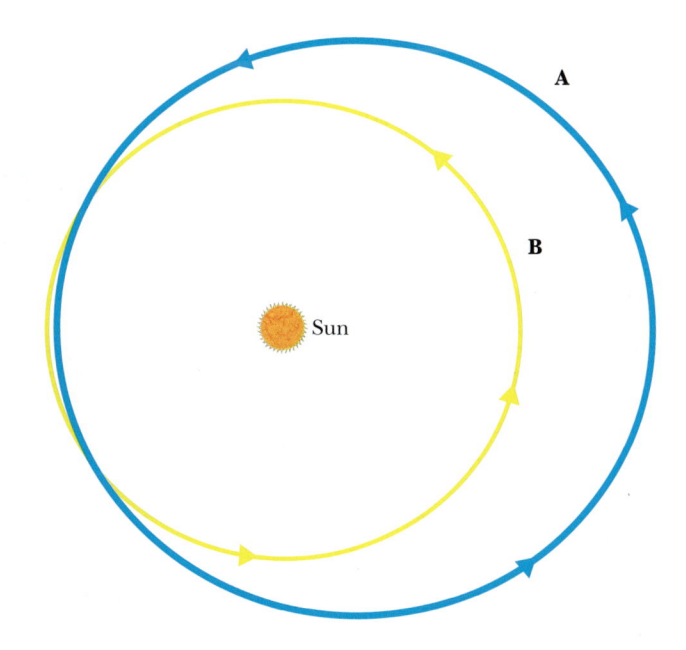

The coloured lines labelled A and B in the diagram above show the orbital paths of Neptune and Pluto.

(f) Copy out the diagram above and examine the orbital paths. Using the information in the table at the top of this page, identify Pluto and Neptune in your diagram.

(g) A school textbook published in 2003 states that 'Pluto is the furthest planet away from the sun'. Evaluate this statement and give two reasons why it may be considered to be untrue.

5. Give an account of a theory to explain the origins of our universe. What evidence is there to support the theory?

36 Earth and Other Planets

Review Questions

1. Earth can be compared with other planets in terms of mass. Give three other ways in which Earth can be compared with other planets.
   (a) _____
   (b) _____
   (c) _____

2. How would a scientist calculate the relative mass of different planets?
   _____

3. All planets generate a gravitational force. Where in a planet is the gravitational force the strongest? _____

4. What is meant by the terms (a) inner planet (b) outer planet?
   (a) _____
   (b) _____

5. What are the names of the four rocky planets of our solar system?
   _____

6. What are the names of the four gas planets of our solar system?
   _____

7. Why do objects on the moon fall more slowly than they do on Earth?
   _____

8. How long does it take Earth to make one complete rotation around its own axis?
   _____

9. How long does it take Earth to make one complete revolution of the sun?
   _____

Knowledge and Understanding

1. The mass of Earth is approximately 6×10^{24} kg. Calculate the approximate mass of the following planets based on their relative masses:

   > **Example:** The relative mass of Mercury is 0.0553
   > Mass of Mercury = Relative mass of Mercury x Mass of Earth
   > $\qquad\qquad\quad = 0.0553 \times 6 \times 10^{24}$ kg.
   > Approximate mass of Mercury = 0.332×10^{24} kg.

Planet	Relative Mass
Mercury	0.0553
Venus	0.815
Mars	0.107
Jupiter	318.0
Saturn	95.2
Uranus	14.5
Neptune	17.1

Earth and Other Planets 36

2. Using the information in the table in Question 1 list the eight planets of our solar system (including Earth) in increasing order of mass.
3. The table below shows data for some of the largest objects in our solar system, with masses, radii and surface gravities shown relative to those of Earth.

Object	Type of object	Relative mass	Relative radius	Relative surface gravity
Sun	Star	333,000	109	28
Jupiter	Planet	318	11.0	2.53
Saturn	Planet	95.2	9.14	1.06
Uranus	Planet	14.5	3.98	0.90
Neptune	Planet	17.1	3.86	1.14
Earth	**Planet**	**1**	**1**	**1**
Venus	Planet	0.815	0.950	0.905
Mars	Planet	0.107	0.532	0.38
Ganymede	Moon of Jupiter	0.0248	0.413	0.15
Titan	Moon of Saturn	0.0225	0.404	0.14
Mercury	Planet	0.0553	0.383	0.38
Callisto	Moon of Jupiter	0.0180	0.378	0.126
Io	Moon of Jupiter	0.0150	0.286	0.183
Moon	Moon of Earth	0.0123	0.273	0.166
Europa	Moon of Jupiter	0.00803	0.245	0.134
Triton	Moon of Neptune	0.00359	0.212	0.0797
Pluto	Dwarf planet	0.0022	0.186	0.062
Eris	Dwarf planet	0.0027	0.182	0.0677
Titania	Moon of Uranus	0.00059	0.124	0.0385

(a) Are these objects listed in order of mass, in order of radius or in order of gravity?

(b) After analysing the data presented above, John concludes that surface gravity decreases as the mass of the object decreases. Is John justified in his conclusion? Explain your answer.

(c) After analysing the data presented above, Ann concludes that surface gravity decreases as the radius of the object decreases. Is Ann justified in her conclusion? Explain your answer.

(d) A scientist wishes to use the data given above to calculate the density of each of the eight planets. Explain how the scientist would calculate the density of each planet. (Note: The volume of a sphere can be calculated using the measurement of its radius.)

(e) After calculating the densities of the eight planets, the scientist is able to place each of the planets into one of two groups, the gas giants (Jupiter, Neptune, Saturn and Uranus) and the rocky planets (Earth, Mars, Mercury and Venus). Which group of planets do you expect to have the greater densities? Explain your answer.

(f) What will happen to the weight of a spacecraft as it leaves Earth, travels through space and arrives at Mars?

(g) Define the word 'planet' in such a way that it includes objects such as Earth, Mars and Jupiter but does not include objects such as Titania, Pluto or the sun.

37 The Earth, Sun and Moon

Review Questions

1. What is the correct alignment during a solar eclipse?
   (a) Sun – Moon – Earth ☐
   (b) Earth – Mars – Moon ☐
   (c) Sun – Earth – Moon ☐
   (d) Moon – Sun – Earth ☐

2. Tides on Earth are affected by the gravitational force(s) of:
   (a) The moon only ☐
   (b) The moon and the sun only ☐
   (c) Earth, the moon and the sun ☐
   (d) Earth and the moon only ☐

3. What term is used to describe the moon when the illuminated area appears to be increasing?
   _____

4. What term is used to describe the moon when the illuminated area appears to be decreasing?
   _____

5. Earth <u>rotates</u> as it <u>revolves</u> around the sun. Explain the difference between the underlined terms. _____
   _____

6. The image below shows Earth at four different positions in its annual orbit of the sun. Which season would be experienced in the northern hemisphere when Earth is in position:
   (A) _____
   (B) _____
   (C) _____
   (D) _____

7. Which season would be experienced in the southern hemisphere when Earth is in position:
   (A) _____
   (B) _____
   (C) _____
   (D) _____

The Earth, Sun and Moon   37

Knowledge and Understanding

1. Explain why night and day occur on Earth.
2. Draw a diagram to illustrate the shape of the orbit of Earth around the sun.
3. Explain how the tilt of Earth's axis causes the seasons in the northern hemisphere.

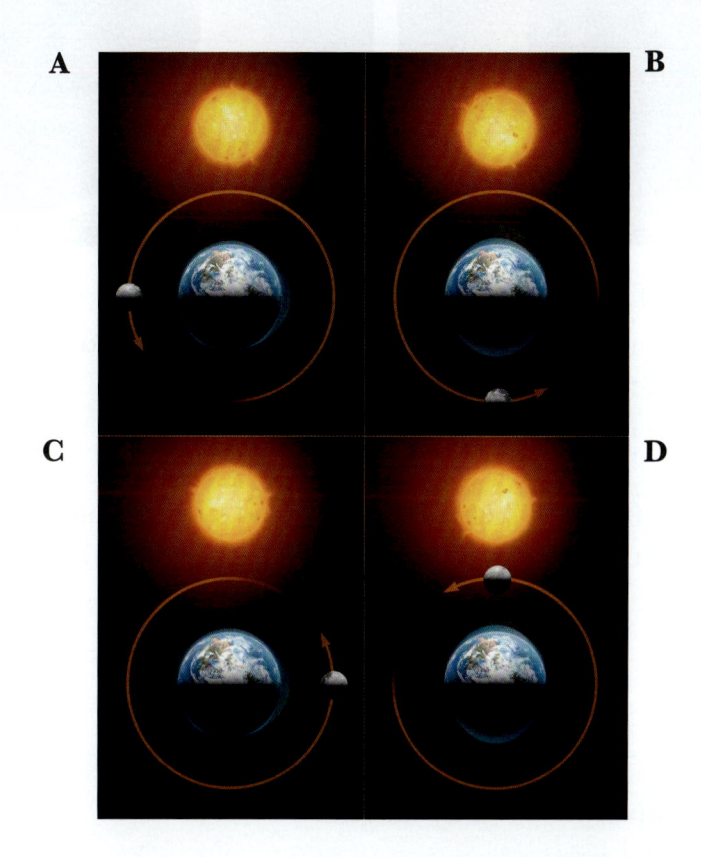

4. The image above illustrates the relative positions of Earth, the sun and the moon at four different stages in the lunar cycle. Which phase of the moon is represented by:
   A. _____
   B. _____
   C. _____
   D. _____
5. Spring tides occur when Earth, the moon and the sun are aligned. Which two diagrams in the image above represent the earth-sun-moon system during spring tides?
6. Neap tides occur when the sun and the moon are at a right angle to Earth. Which two diagrams represent the earth-sun-moon system during neap tides?
7. Tidal range is the difference between the height of the water at low tide and high tide. Which type of tide do you think gives the greatest variation: spring tides or neap tides? Give a reason for your answer.
8. What type of tides would you expect when there is a full moon? Give a reason for your answer.
9. What phase would you expect the moon to be in during neap tides? Give a reason for your answer.

A

B

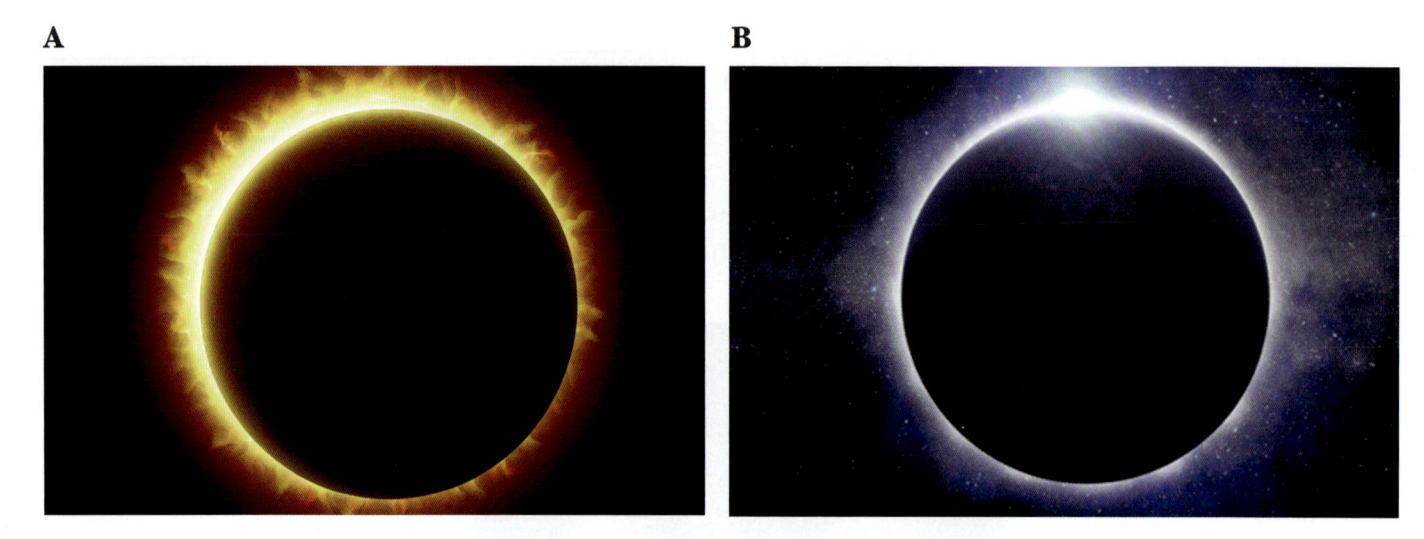

10. The photographs A and B above show two types of solar eclipse: a **total** eclipse when the sun is completely blocked out and a partial eclipse when the sun is not completely blocked out.
    (a) Which photograph represents the total eclipse?
    (b) Which photograph represents the partial eclipse?

11. Day length is the amount of time between sunrise and sunset. The table below gives the times for sunrise and sunset in Belfast, Dublin and Cork on 21 June 2014:

	Sunrise	Sunset	Day length
Belfast	4.47 a.m.	21.04 p.m.	
Dublin	4.57 a.m.	21.57 p.m.	
Cork	5.14 a.m.	21.57 p.m.	

(a) Calculate the day length for each of the three cities
(b) List the three cities in increasing order of day length.
(c) Account for the differences in day length in these three cities.
(d) June 21 is the summer solstice in the northern hemisphere. It is often referred to as the longest day of the year. Do you think that this is a scientifically accurate way to refer to the solstice? Give a reason for your answer.
(e) Sydney, Australia is in the southern hemisphere. What do you think is the date for the winter solstice in Sydney? Give a reason for your answer.
(f) Draw a diagram of Earth and the sun on the day of the summer solstice in the northern hemisphere. Clearly indicate Earth's axis in your diagram. What is unique about the relative positions of Earth and the sun on this day?

38 Space Exploration

Review Questions

1. Name two technologies we use that were originally developed for space exploration.
   (a) _____
   (b) _____

2. What advantage do satellites have for communication?
   _____

3. The International Space Station (ISS) is a project on which many countries work together. When was the ISS launched? _____

4. Identify three areas of research that the ISS is used for.
   (a) _____
   (b) _____
   (c) _____

5. There are more than 21,000 pieces of man-made debris in space.
   (a) Suggest where these pieces of debris may have come from.
   _____

   (b) What danger do these pieces of debris pose for further space exploration?
   _____

   (c) What danger can these pieces of debris pose if they return to Earth's gravitational field?
   _____

Knowledge and Understanding

1. Read the following two articles and answer the questions.

Case Study   Mars One Project

Article 1   Mars One Project

Fig. 1 An artist's impression of what Mars One's first human colony on Mars might look like.

The goal of the Mars One project is to establish a human settlement on Mars. While complex, the Mars One Mission is possible.

The science and technology required to place humans on Mars exists today. Much of what was learned from the space stations Skylab,

Mir and the International Space Station has resulted in vital data and experience which can be applied to living on Mars.

Basic elements required for a living system are already present on Mars, so we need to send more tools and equipment rather than raw elements. For example, the location for the first Mars One settlement is selected for the water content of the soil there. Water can be made available to the settlement for hygiene, drinking and farming, and can be used to produce oxygen by electrolysis. Mars also has ample natural sources of nitrogen, the main element (nearly 80%) in the air we breathe. Martian soil will cover the outpost to block cosmic radiation.

The astronauts will be able to create habitation for themselves and for new crews using local materials. For a long time, the supply requests from the outpost will be for computers, clothing and complex spare parts, which cannot be readily reproduced with the limited technology on Mars.

No new major developments or inventions are needed to make the mission plan a reality. Each stage of Mars One mission plan uses existing, tested and available technology.

Adapted from www.mars-one.com/mission

Article 2

Mars One Mission Currently Not Feasible, MIT Study Finds

Bad news for anyone who was looking forward to humans colonising Mars anytime soon.

A recent Massachusetts Institute of Technology (MIT) study has found that plans for Mars One – that scary-sounding Dutch mission to send a bunch of Earthlings on a one-way trip to colonise the Red Planet – are currently not realistic.

'One of the biggest claims made by the Mars One team is that absolutely no new technology needs to be developed for the success of their mission,' said aerospace engineer Sydney Do, who led the study. 'We found that there are several cases – for systems like the environmental control and life support – where that's just not true.'

According to the study, there are a number of reasons Mars One might be destined for disaster, as the plans stand right now.

One problem, the researchers found, was that it would take an unsustainable amount of

Fig. 2 An artist's impression of what Mars One's first human colony on Mars might look like.

money and resources to resupply the growing colony with the spare parts it would eventually need.

'The mission's plan relies on a steady resupply stream – bringing replacements like filters, pumps, motors – for when something inevitably breaks,' Mr Do said. 'As the colony expands, you find that the sheer mass of the spare parts you're transporting explodes and becomes a bigger and bigger part of what you send to Mars each time you launch.'

The study also found that with all the plants

Space Exploration

required to feed Mars One's participants, the colony would eventually contain excess levels of oxygen, which could pose a fire risk.

Mr Do said that here on Earth we have technologies to remove excess oxygen from the atmosphere, but 'as far as [his study] could find, this issue of needing to remove oxygen has never been mentioned in any of the Mars One plans.'

Mars One's site still states that the plan is to ship crews of four out to Mars every two years, starting in 2024. Maybe Buzz Aldrin, who is in favour of colonising Mars, needs to step in and give everybody some guidance.

From betabeat.com/2014/10/mars-one-mission-is-currently-infeasible-mit-study-finds

Questions

Both of these articles are about the Mars One project. The first is an extract from the Mars One website. The second is from BetaBeat, a news and opinion blog run by the *New York Observer* newspaper. Answer the following questions:

(a) Identify the difficulties of the Mars One mission given in each article.
(b) Identify one specific aspect of the Mars One mission where these articles disagree.
(c) Compare these two articles under these headings:
   (i) Bias   (ii) Scientific content
(d) The second article mentions research undertaken by the Massachusetts Institute of Technology (MIT). Identify the information that is used in this article to support the argument that the plans 'are currently not realistic'.
(e) From your reading of these articles do you think the Mars One mission is realistic? Refer to the content of both articles in your answer.
(f) State whether or not you would be interested in being on this mission and outline your reasons.

2. The table below lists some of the known health risks associated with different stages of space flight. Read it and then answer the questions below.

Part of spaceflight	Health risks
Launch	Possible loss of consciousness
10 minutes after launch	Nausea due to motion sickness
2 days into mission	Build-up of fluid in upper body

Part of spaceflight	Health risks
1 week into mission	Muscle and bone loss
2 weeks into mission	Sleep deprivation
1 year into mission	Increased susceptibility to disease

Questions

(a) There is a gym on board the ISS. Which health risks could be reduced by the astronauts using the gym?
(b) Suggest activities that could reduce the loss of bone and muscle mass.
(c) Which of the risks listed above do you think could be more challenging for missions to Mars than for shorter missions?

39 Cycles on Earth

Review Questions

1. Look at this diagram of the water cycle and answer the questions below.

   (a) Name the stages 1-4.

   1. _____ .
   2. _____ .
   3. _____ .
   4. _____ .

   (b) How are clouds formed? _____
   (c) What is the name of the process that causes water to evaporate from the surface of a leaf?
   _____

   (d) List three different forms of precipitation. (i) _____
   (ii) _____
   (iii) _____

   (e) Name two places where fresh water will collect when it has fallen as precipitation.

   (i) _____
   (ii) _____

   (f) Where does fresh water flow to? _____

Cycles on Earth — 39

2. Examine this diagram of the carbon cycle on Earth and answer the questions below.

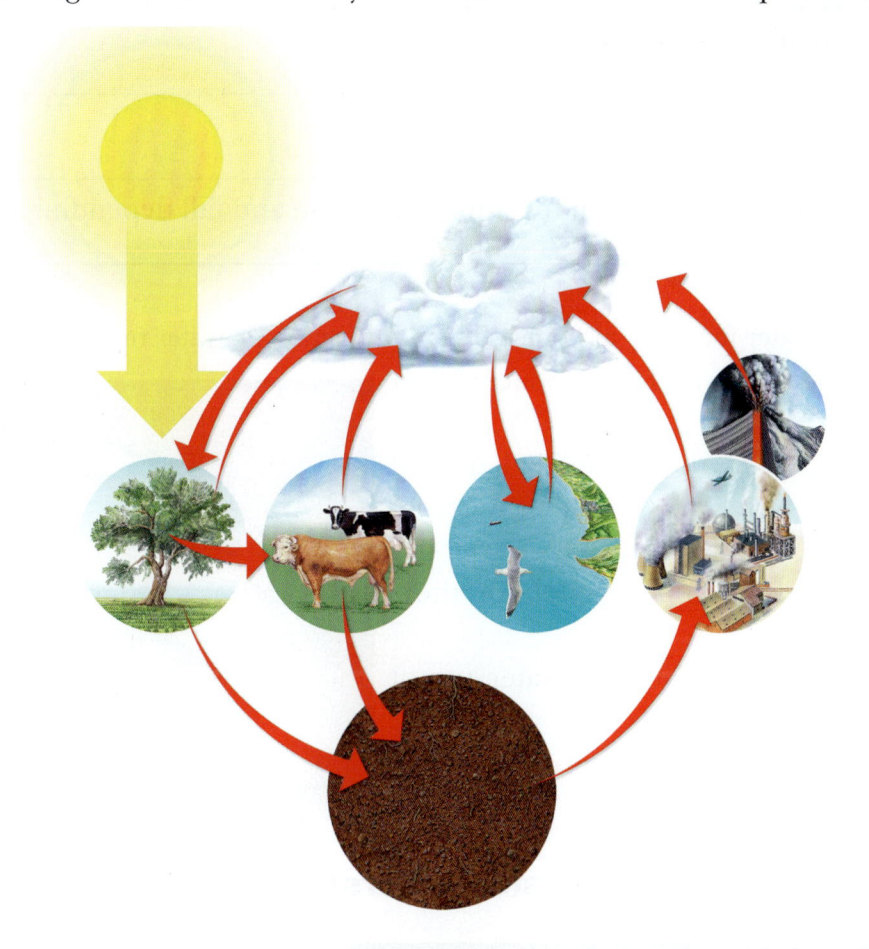

(a) Compounds that contain carbon are called _____ compounds.

(b) What is the name of the carbon-containing compound that living things exhale?
   _____

(c) What process involving the intake of carbon dioxide occurs in green plants?
   _____

(d) List two types of fossil fuel.
   (i) _____
   (ii) _____

(e) Burning fossil fuels releases water vapour and which other gas?
   _____

(f) Outline the role of decomposers in the carbon cycle.
   _____

(g) List two ways in which carbon dioxide is removed from the atmosphere.
   (i) _____
   (ii) _____

(h) List two ways in which carbon dioxide is released into the atmosphere.
   (i) _____
   (ii) _____

(i) Give two examples of where carbon compounds are stored on Earth.
   (i) _____
   (ii) _____

(j) Write the word equation for photosynthesis.

(k) Write the word equation for respiration.

(l) Write the word equation for combustion of a fossil fuel.

(m) Explain why carbon dioxide levels in the atmosphere rise and fall depending on the season.

3. Ireland has introduced water metering in homes. The introduction of water meters may cause people to think more carefully about the way they use water in their day-to-day lives.
   (a) Identify two activities in the home that do not require treated tap water, for example, watering plants.
   (b) How could a household collect water for these activities?
   (c) Identify ways of reducing your tap water use at home.
   (d) Why is it important to conserve water?

Knowledge and Understanding

Case Study   The Case of the Missing Carbon

Ocean waters gather it in. But what happens when the planet's great carbon recycling system goes off course?

It's there on a monitor: the forest is breathing. Steven Wofsy (an atmospheric scientist at Harvard University) unlocks a shed in a Massachusetts woodland and enters a room stuffed with equipment. The machinery monitors the vital functions of a small section of Harvard Forest in the centre of Massachusetts. The readings show the carbon dioxide concentration just above the treetops near the shed, where instruments on a 30-metre-high tower monitor the air. The numbers are running surprisingly low for the beginning of the 21st century: around 360 parts per million, 10 less than the global average. That's because of the trees. Basking in the sunshine, they inhale carbon dioxide and turn it into leaves and wood.

This patch of pine, oak, and maple is undoing a tiny bit of a great global change driven by humans. Start the car, turn on a light, turn up the thermostat, or do just about anything, and you add carbon dioxide to the atmosphere. The coal, oil and natural gas that drive the industrial world's economy all contain carbon inhaled by plants hundreds of millions of years ago – carbon that is now returning to the atmosphere through smokestacks and exhaust pipes, joining emissions from forests burned to clear land in poorer countries

Carbon dioxide is foremost in a list of gases produced by human activity that increase the atmosphere's ability to trap heat. Few scientists doubt that this greenhouse warming of the atmosphere is already taking hold. Melting glaciers, earlier springs and a steady rise in global average temperature are just some of the signs.

By rights it should be worse. Each year humans dump roughly 8 billion metric tons of carbon into the atmosphere, 6.5 billion from fossil fuels and 1.5 billion from deforestation. But less than half that total, 3.2 billion tons, remains in the atmosphere to warm the planet. Where is the missing carbon? 'It's a major mystery, if you think about it,' says Wofsy. His research site in Harvard Forest is apparently not the only place where nature is breathing deep and helping to save us from ourselves. Forests, grasslands and the waters of the oceans must be acting as carbon sinks. They steal back a lot of the carbon dioxide we release, slowing its build-up in the atmosphere and slowing the effects on climate. Who can complain? No one, for now. But the problem is that scientists can't be sure that this blessing will last, or as the globe continues to warm, it might even change to a curse if forests and other ecosystems change from being carbon sinks to sources, releasing more carbon into the atmosphere than they absorb. The doubts have sent researchers into forests and rangelands, out to the tundra and to sea, to track down and understand the missing carbon.

By Tim Appenzellar, *National Geographic (adapted)*

Questions

(a) Where is the research being carried out?
(b) Levels of what gas are being recorded?
(c) The article uses the term 'inhale' when describing the intake of carbon dioxide by the trees. Why is this an incorrect term to use?
(d) What process using carbon dioxide occurs in the trees?
(e) List three ways mentioned in this article in which human activity adds carbon dioxide to the atmosphere.
(f) Name two effects of the warming of the planet.
(g) How many metric tons of carbon (on average) are dumped into the atmosphere per year by humans?
(h) How much of this is caused by deforestation?
(i) If only 3.2 billion tons of carbon remain in the atmosphere, give your suggestion as to where the 'missing' carbon could be.
(j) Based on the evidence in this article, what steps can humans take to remove more CO_2 from the atmosphere?

40 Climate Change

Review Questions

1. How does the sun influence Earth's climate? _____
   _____

2. How do greenhouse gases act like an insulating blanket around Earth? _____
   _____
   _____

3. How does the movement of air from the equator to the poles affect the climate in Ireland?
   _____
   _____

4. How do ocean currents, like the Gulf Stream, affect the climate in Ireland? _____
   _____

5. How does the ozone layer protect Earth? _____
   _____

6. List the natural greenhouse gases present in Earth's atmosphere. _____
   _____
   _____

7. What factors have caused climate change on Earth in the past? _____
   _____

8. Why do you think some scientists believe that climate change is a natural phenomenon?
   _____
   _____

9. Why has the amount of fossil fuels being burned increased so much since the 19th century?
   _____

10. List the activities that cause carbon dioxide to be released into the atmosphere.
    _____
    _____

11. List the activities that cause methane to be released into the atmosphere.
    _____
    _____

12. List the activities that cause nitrous oxide to be released into the atmosphere.
    _____
    _____

Climate Change 40

13. This graph uses data from ice cores to show the changing levels of carbon dioxide and methane over the last 1,000 years. What is the relationship between the levels of carbon dioxide and methane in the atmosphere since the year 1000 AD?

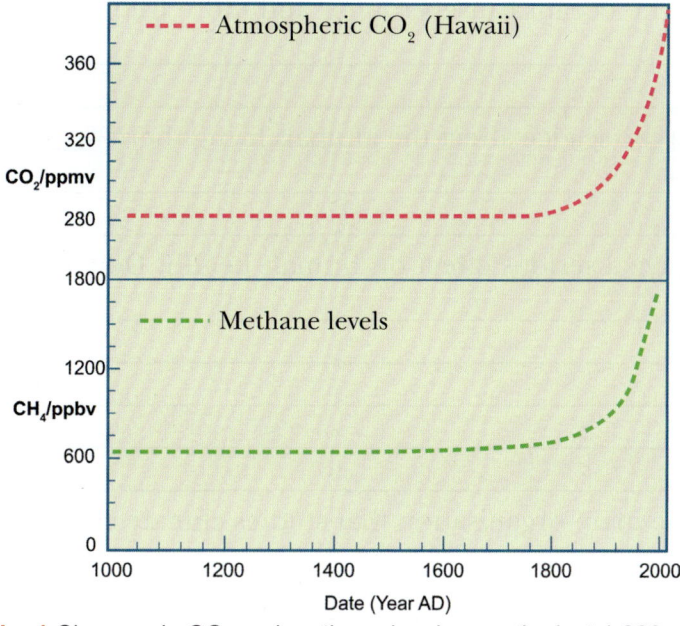

Fig. 1 Changes in CO_2 and methane levels over the last 1,000 years.

_____
_____

14. Analyse the following two graphs. What appears to be the relationship between the percentage of carbon dioxide in the atmosphere and global average temperatures?

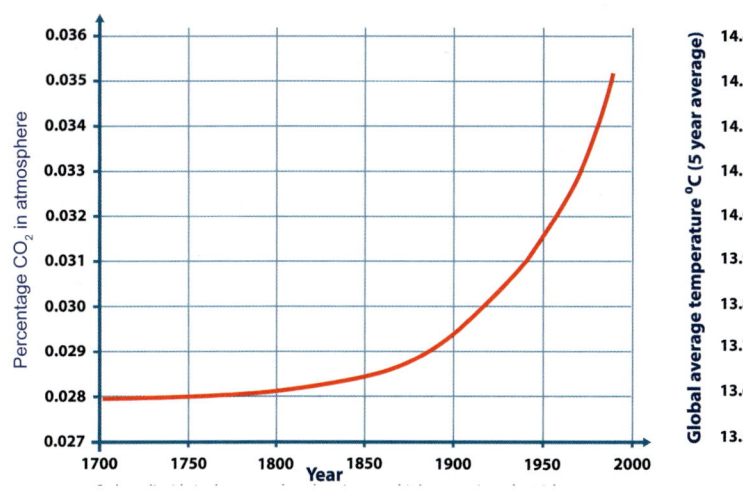

Fig. 2 Percentage CO_2 in the atmosphere.

Fig. 3 Global average temperatures.

_____
_____
_____
_____

15. How does climate change affect life on land? _____
_____
_____

16. How does climate change affect life in the oceans?

17. How does warming of the oceans cause stronger and more frequent storms?

18. How does declining Arctic sea ice affect the animals living there?

19. Climate change will have a serious effect on human health. Do you agree with this statement? Explain your answer.

20. What is the name of the main organisation that studies climate change?

21. List four ways that climate change may affect Ireland.

22. What is a carbon footprint?

23. List at least five small changes that you could make to reduce your carbon footprint.

24. What is the Kyoto Protocol?

25. Nations attending the United Nations Climate Change Conference (UNCCC) in Paris in 2015 agreed to a number of measures to reduce climate change. Research what these measures were, and list them.

26. Pick one of the measures from your list in Question 25 and evaluate how it will contribute to reducing climate change.

27. List two initiatives introduced in Ireland to try to reduce the emission of greenhouse gases.

28. Pick one of the two initiatives from Question 27 and outline how this will reduce our greenhouse gas emissions.

Climate Change 40

Knowledge and Understanding

Read the following two articles and answer the questions.

Case Study: Carbon Dioxide in the atmosphere and climate change

Article 1

Climate change: How do we know?

The earth's climate has changed throughout history. Just in the last 650,000 years there have been seven cycles of glacial growth and retreat, with the sudden end of the last ice age about 7,000 years ago marking the beginning of the modern climate era — and of human civilisation. Most of these climate changes are because of very small variations in Earth's orbit that change the amount of solar energy our planet receives.

> "Scientific evidence for warming of the climate system is unequivocal."
> *- Intergovernmental Panel on Climate Change*

The current warming trend is of particular significance because most of it is very likely human-induced and proceeding at a rate that is unprecedented in the past 1,300 years.

Satellites and other technological advances have enabled scientists to see the big picture, collecting many different types of information about our planet and its climate on a global scale. Studying this climate data collected over many years reveals the signals of a changing climate.

Ice cores drawn from Greenland, Antarctica and tropical mountain glaciers show that the earth's climate responds to changes in solar output, changes in the earth's orbit, and in greenhouse gas levels. They also show that in the past, large changes in climate have happened very quickly: in tens of years, not in millions or even thousands.

All three major global surface temperature reconstructions show that Earth has warmed since 1880. Most of this warming has occurred since the 1970s, with the 20 warmest years having occurred since 1981 and with all 10 of the warmest years occurring in the past 12 years. Even though the 2000s witnessed a solar output decline resulting in an unusually deep solar minimum in 2007-2009, surface temperatures continue to increase.

climate.nasa.gov/evidence (adapted)

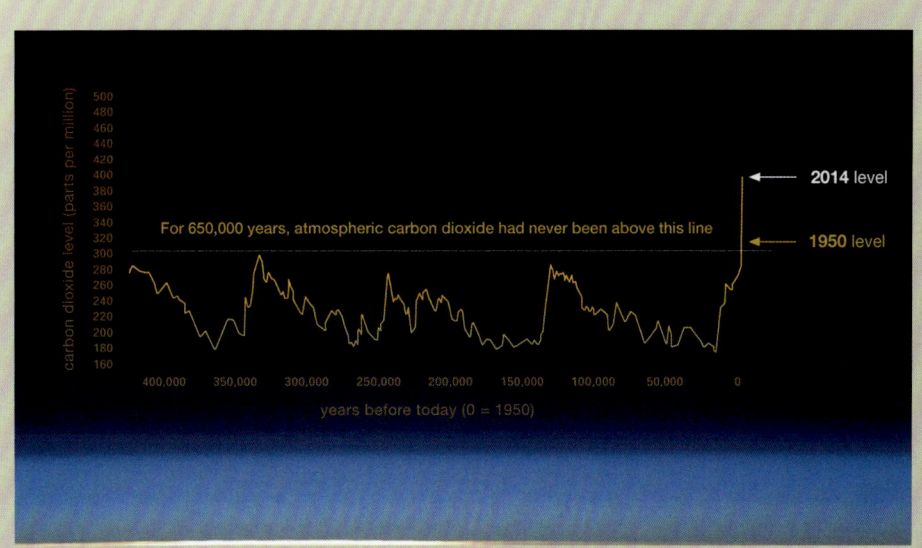

Case Study: Global warming and climate change

Article 2

No Need to Panic About Global Warming

There is an increasing number of scientists who publicly disagree that man-made global warming is happening. However, many young scientists secretly say that while they have serious doubts about the global warming message, they are afraid to speak up for fear of not being promoted – or worse. They have good reason to worry. In 2003, Dr Chris de Freitas, the editor of the journal *Climate Research*, dared to publish an article with the politically incorrect (but factually correct) conclusion that the recent warming is not unusual when compared to climate changes over the past thousand years. The international warming establishment quickly mounted a determined campaign to have Dr de Freitas let go from his job. Fortunately, Dr de Freitas was able to keep his job.

This is not the way science is supposed to work, but we have seen it before – for example when in the 1930s in the Soviet Union, Soviet biologists who revealed that they believed in genes were fired from their jobs. Many were sent to labour camps and some were condemned to death.

Why is there so much passion about global warming? Alarmism over climate is of great benefit to many, providing government funding for academic research and a reason for government organisations to grow. Alarmism also offers an excuse for governments to raise taxes, taxpayer-funded subsidies for businesses and a lure for big donations to charitable foundations promising to save the planet.

Speaking for many scientists and engineers who have looked carefully and independently at the science of climate, we have a message to any candidate for public office: There is no compelling scientific argument for drastic action to 'decarbonise' the world's economy. Even if one accepts the inflated climate forecasts of the IPCC, aggressive greenhouse-gas control policies are not justified economically.

From a letter to the Wall Street Journal (adapted)

Questions

1. Look at the sources of these two articles. Which one do you think is a scientific organisation and which one is a financial newspaper?
2. Based on the information in these articles, list two factors that have caused Earth's climate to change in the past?
3. What evidence has been presented to support the claim that Earth is currently warming up?
4. What type of human activities could be leading to the 'human-induced' warming trend?
5. Why do you think the *Wall Street Journal* would publish an article that argues there is no need to reduce our carbon emissions (decarbonise the world economy)?
6. Do you think either of these articles are biased? Justify your answer.

Climate Change 40

Analyse and Interpret

1. Analyse Figs. 1, 2 and 3. Answer the questions that follow.

   Note: The purple line shows a prediction of what will happen if we successfully reduce our greenhouse gas emissions.

   The red line shows a prediction of what may happen if we continue as we have been doing!

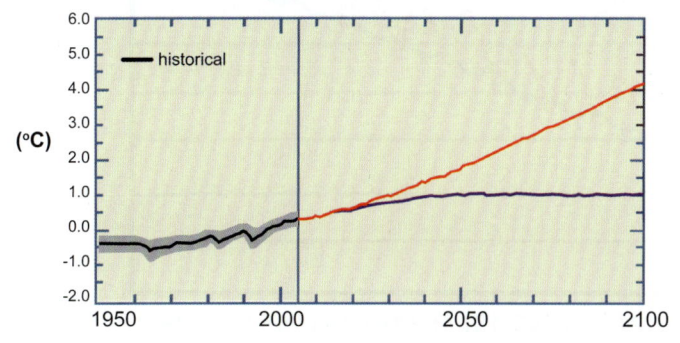

Fig. (1) Global average surface temperature change.

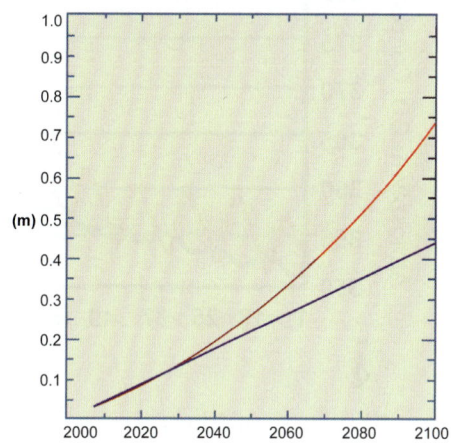

Fig. (2) Global average sea level rise.

Fig. (3) Global ocean surface pH.

Source: *IPCC Fifth Climate Change Report 2013*

Questions

(a) How much are average global temperatures expected to increase between 1950 and 2100 if humans do not reduce their greenhouse gas emissions?

(b) How much are global temperatures expected to rise by 2100 if humans reduce their greenhouse gas emissions?

(c) What can be done to help prevent global temperatures rising as predicted in Fig (1)?

(d) What is the highest predicted sea level rise by 2100 according to Fig (2)?

(e) What impact will a rise in sea levels have on people living in low-lying coastal areas?

(f) Give one cause of rising sea levels on Earth.

(g) What was the global ocean surface pH in 1950?

(h) What is the global ocean surface pH at present?

(i) What is the lowest expected drop in ocean pH between 1950 and 2100? Give a reason for the estimated further drop in ocean pH in the future

(j) What effect will further acidification of the ocean have on the organisms living there?

2. Carefully examine the graph below:

Comparison of atmospheric CO_2 concentrations from January 1990 to December 2009 at the South Pole (SPO) and Mauna Lao, Hawaii (MLO)

[Graph: x-axis shows Number of months since January 1990 (1 to 229); y-axis shows Atmosphere CO_2 Concentration/ ppm (350 to 395). Two lines: SPO (blue) and MLO (red), both showing rising trends with seasonal oscillations.]

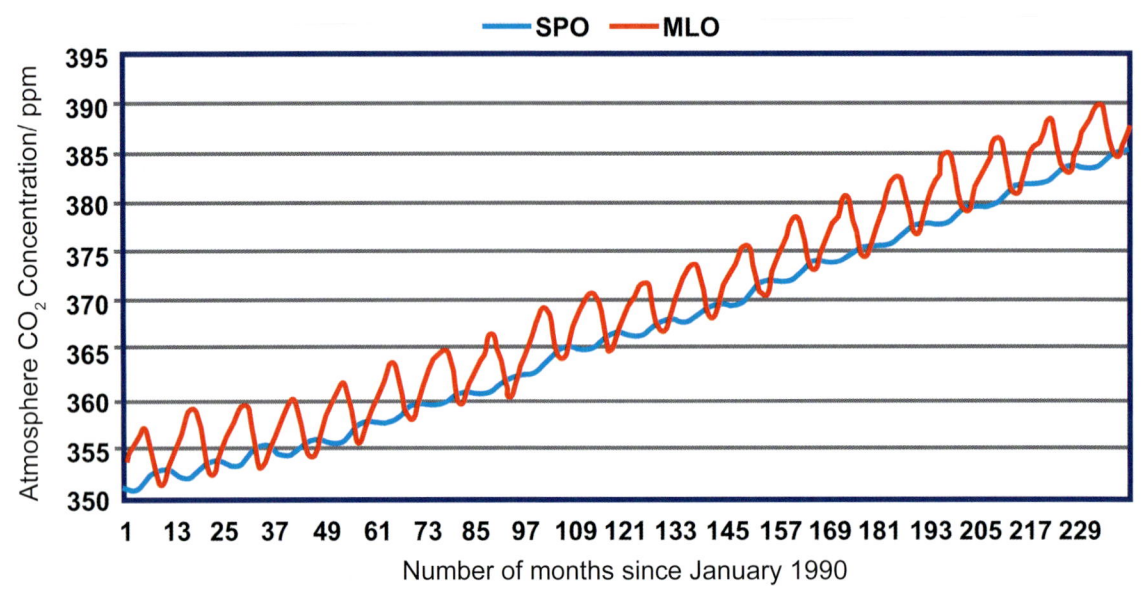

These 20 years of data from the South Pole and Mauna Loa, Hawaii show that CO_2 concentration in the atmosphere is rising. Within a single year, the level goes through a clear maximum and minimum before rising again to a higher peak level the following year. The cycle is more noticeable in Hawaii than at the South Pole.

In Hawaii (in the northern hemisphere) the levels rise throughout November/December until April/May when they begin to fall again. The pattern of this timing is the opposite at the South Pole.

Questions

In Hawaii
1. Which season has the highest levels of atmospheric CO_2?
2. Why are atmospheric CO_2 levels high at this time of the year?
3. Which season has the lowest levels of atmospheric CO_2?
4. Why are atmospheric CO_2 levels low at this time of the year?

In the South Pole
5. Why do you think the fluctuations in levels of atmospheric CO_2 are the opposite of those in Hawaii?
6. Why do you think the seasonal changes in CO_2 levels are less dramatic than those in Hawaii?
7. How many years are represented on this graph?
8. Calculate the average increase in CO_2 concentrations at Mauna Loa in parts per million (ppm) over this time frame.
9. Calculate the average increase in CO_2 concentration at the South Pole in parts per million (ppm) over this time frame.
10. Based on this data, what conclusion can you make about the levels of CO_2 in Earth's atmosphere.

41 Energy Sources

Review Questions

1. Give two examples of fossil fuels. **(a)** _____ **(b)** _____

2. Why are fossil fuels non-renewable sources of energy? _____
_____

3. How are fossil fuels formed? _____
_____

4. What is a renewable energy source? _____
_____

5. Why is wind energy a renewable source of energy? _____
_____

6. Give two other examples of renewable energy. **(a)** _____ **(b)** _____

7. What is nuclear fission? _____
_____

8. List the sources of energy that can be used for the activities A–D:

Activity	Source of Energy
A. Heating	
B. Transport	
C. Cooking	
D. Generating electricity	

9. (a) Match the types of power station A–F with the energy sources 1–6.

Power station	Energy source
A. Hydroelectric	1. Heat released from the combustion of fossil fuels
B. Geothermal	2. The motion energy of moving water
C. Coal-fired power station	3. Energy from sunlight
D. Wind farm	4. Heat released from a nuclear fission reaction involving radioactive uranium
E. Solar cells	5. Heat from deep within the earth
F. Nuclear power	6. Wind

(b) Write R beside renewable sources of energy.
(c) Write NR beside the non-renewable sources of energy.

10. Which energy sources must be mined or drilled to extract them? _____

11. Which energy sources are available without mining or drilling into the earth? _____

12. List the energy sources that cause pollution in their extraction. _____

13. Which energy sources release pollution into the atmosphere when burned? _____

14. Which energy sources produce carbon dioxide when burned? _____

15. Which energy sources do not produce carbon dioxide? _____

16. What forms of energy production do not require a fuel? _____

17. What conditions are required to produce energy from the sources (a) and (b) below?

(a) Wind turbines   (b) Solar panels

Energy Sources 41

18. What are the advantages of using (a) hydroelectric power and (b) geothermal power to produce energy?

(a) Hydroelectric power

(b) Geothermal power

19. List the advantages and disadvantages of using (a) coal and (b) oil to produce energy.

(a) Coal _____
_____
_____
_____

(b) Oil _____
_____
_____
_____

20. Nuclear power stations produce huge amounts of energy without producing carbon emissions. Suggest two reasons why some people oppose nuclear power.

(a) _____
_____
_____
_____

(b) _____
_____
_____
_____

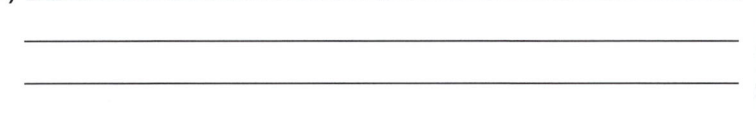

145

Analyse and Interpret

Examine the three graphs below and answer the questions that follow.

World Population 1965 - 2050

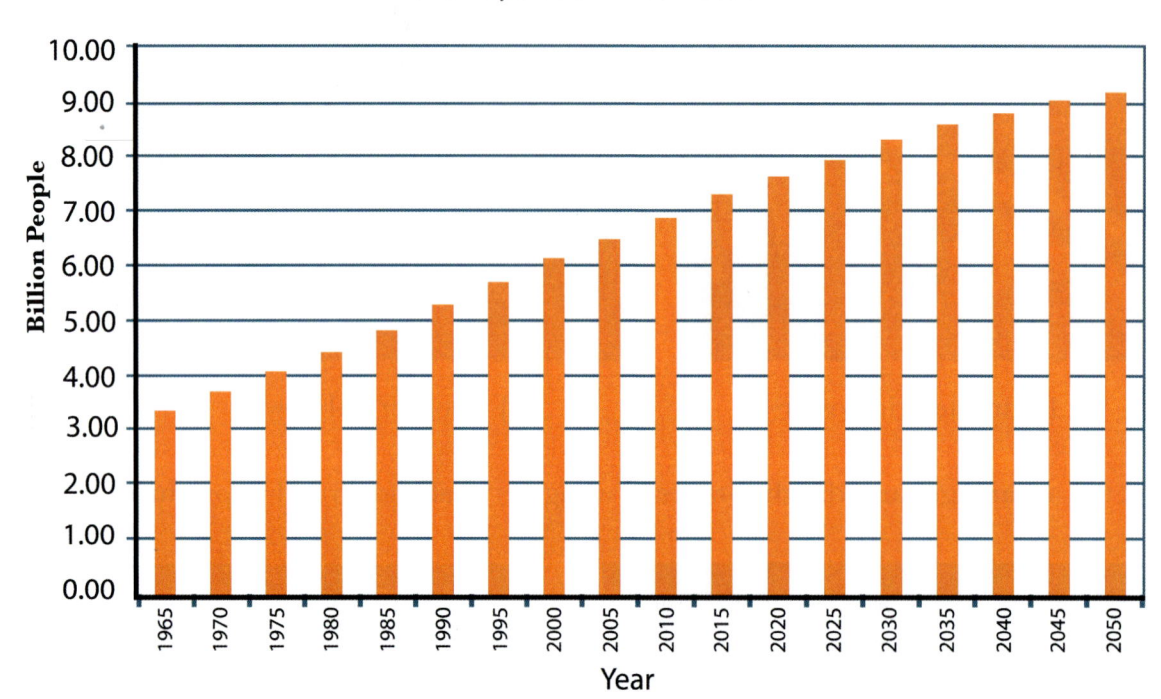

Fig. 1 The world's increasing population, 1965–2050.

World carbon dioxide emissions

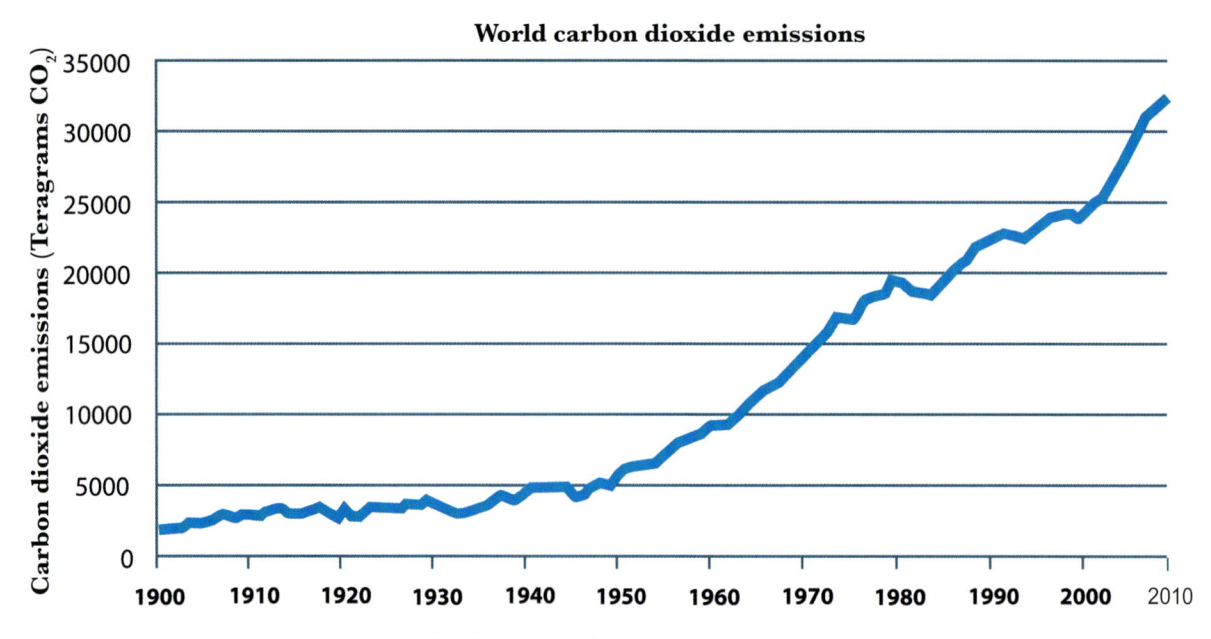

Fig. 2 World carbon dioxide emissions 1900–2010.

Energy Sources 41

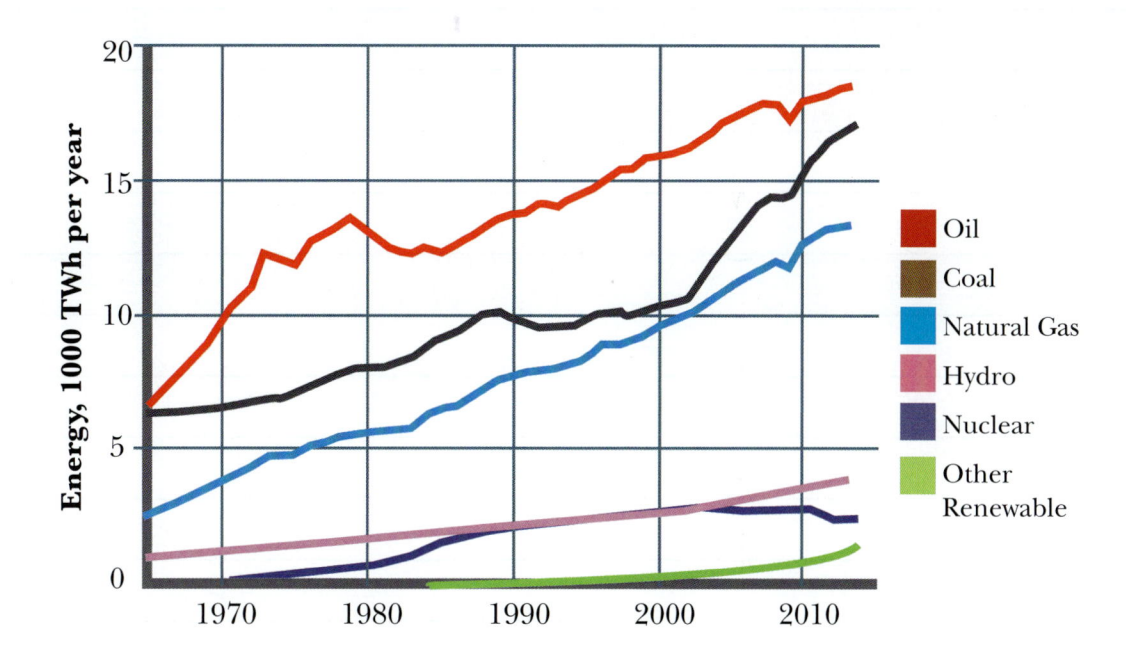

Fig. 3 World energy consumption 1970–2010.

1. How did the world's population change between 1970 and 2010?
2. How did the world's energy consumption change between 1970 and 2010?
3. Why do you think world CO_2 emissions have increased in the same time frame?
4. The world's population is predicted to reach 9 billion by 2050. How do you think this will affect energy consumption?
5. What will happen to the levels of carbon dioxide emissions produced if we continue to rely on fossil fuels to provide energy?
6. What effect will increasing CO_2 emissions have on Earth?
7. How do you think global energy demands could be met in the future without further harm to the environment?

Notes

Notes

Notes

Notes

The Periodic Table

	1	2											3	4	5	6	7	8
n=1	1 **H** Hydrogen 1																	2 **He** Helium 4
n=2	3 **Li** Lithium 7	4 **Be** Beryllium 10											5 **B** Boron 11	6 **C** Carbon 12	7 **N** Nitrogen 14	8 **O** Oxygen 16	9 **F** Fluorine 19	10 **Ne** Neon 20
n=3	11 **Na** Sodium 23	12 **Mg** Magnesium 24											13 **Al** Aluminium 27	14 **Si** Silicon 28	15 **P** Phosphorus 31	16 **S** Sulfur 32	17 **Cl** Chlorine 35	18 **Ar** Argon 40
n=4	19 **K** Potassium 39	20 **Ca** Calcium 40	21 **Sc** Scandium 45	22 **Ti** Titanium 48	23 **V** Vanadium 51	24 **Cr** Chromium 52	25 **Mn** Manganese 55	26 **Fe** Iron 56	27 **Co** Cobalt 59	28 **Ni** Nickel 59	29 **Cu** Copper 64	30 **Zn** Zinc 65	31 **Ga** Gallium 70	32 **Ge** Germanium 73	33 **As** Arsenic 75	34 **Se** Selenium 79	35 **Br** Bromine 80	36 **Kr** Krypton 84
n=5	37 **Rb** Rubidium 85	38 **Sr** Strontium 88	39 **Y** Yttrium 89	40 **Zr** Zirconium 91	41 **Nb** Niobium 93	42 **Mo** Molybdenum 96	43 **Tc** Technetium 99	44 **Ru** Ruthenium 101	45 **Rh** Rhodium 103	46 **Pd** Palladium 106	47 **Ag** Silver 108	48 **Cd** Cadmium 112	49 **In** Indium 115	50 **Sn** Tin 119	51 **Sb** Antimony 122	52 **Te** Tellurium 128	53 **I** Iodine 127	54 **Xe** Xenon 131
n=6	55 **Cs** Caesium 133	56 **Ba** Barium 137	57 **La** Lanthanum 139	72 **Hf** Hafnium 178	73 **Ta** Tantalum 181	74 **W** Tungsten 184	75 **Re** Rhenium 186	76 **Os** Osmium 190	77 **Ir** Iridium 192	78 **Pt** Platinum 195	79 **Au** Gold 197	80 **Hg** Mercury 201	81 **Tl** Thallium 204	82 **Pb** Lead 207	83 **Bi** Bismuth 209	84 **Po** Polonium 210	85 **At** Astatine 210	86 **Rn** Radon 222
n=7	87 **Fr** Francium 223	88 **Ra** Radium 226	89 **Ac** Actinium 227	104 **Rf** Rutherfordium	105 **Db** Dubnium	106 **Sg** Seaborgium	107 **Bh** Bohrium	108 **Hs** Hassium	109 **Mt** Meitnerium	110 **Ds** Darmstadtium	111 **Rg** Roentgenium	112 **Cn** Copernicium	113 **Uut** Ununtrium	114 **Fl** Flerovium	115 **Uup** Ununpentium	116 **Lv** Livermorium	117 **Uus** Ununseptium	118 **Uuo** Ununoctium

Key:
- ☐ Metals
- ☐ Metalloids
- ☐ Non-metals